The Manager's Guide to
Program Evaluation

Planning, Contracting, and Managing for Useful Results

Paul W. Mattessich, Ph.D.
Wilder Research

FIELDSTONE
ALLIANCE

SAINT PAUL
MINNESOTA

We thank The David and Lucile Packard Foundation and the
Amherst H. Wilder Foundation for support of this publication.

Copyright © 2003 Fieldstone Alliance

Fieldstone Alliance is committed to strengthening the performance of the nonprofit sector. Through the synergy of its consulting, training, publishing, and research and demonstration projects, Fieldstone Alliance provides solutions to issues facing nonprofits, funders, and the communities they serve. Fieldstone Alliance was formerly Wilder Publishing and Wilder Consulting departments of the Amherst H. Wilder Foundation. For information about other Fieldstone Alliance publications, see the last pages of this book. If you would like more information about Fieldstone Alliance and our services, please contact us at

1-800-274-6024
www.FieldstoneAlliance.org

To learn more about Wilder Research, contact:

Wilder Research
Amherst H. Wilder Foundation
651-280-2700
www.wilder.org/research

Edited by Vincent Hyman
Designed by Kirsten Nielsen

Manufactured in the United States of America
Third printing, February 2008

Limited permission to copy

We have developed this publication to benefit non-profit and community organizations. To enable this, we grant the purchaser of this work limited permission to reproduce forms, charts, graphics, or brief excerpts from the book so long as the reproductions are for direct use by the individual or organization that purchased the book and not for use by others outside the organization. For example, an organization that purchased the book to help its staff or board make plans relevant to the topic of this book may make copies of material from the book to distribute to others in the organization as they plan.

For permission to make multiple copies outside of the permission granted here—for example, for training, for use in a compilation of materials, for public presentation, or to otherwise distribute portions of the book to organizations and individuals that did not purchase the book—please visit the publisher's web site, www.FieldstoneAlliance.org/permissions.

Aside from the limited permission granted here, all other rights not expressly granted here are reserved.

Library of Congress Cataloging-in-Publication Data

Mattessich, Paul W.
  The manager's guide to program evaluation : planning, contracting, and managing for useful results / Paul W. Mattessich.
      p. cm.
Includes bibliographical references and index.
  ISBN-13: 978-0-940069-38-1
  ISBN-10: 0-940069-38-5 (pbk.)
  1. Project management. 2. Management--Evaluation. 3. Evaluation. 4. Evaluation--Methodology. I. Title.
  HD69.P75M3784 2003
  658.4'04--dc21
                            2003009647

About the Author

Paul W. Mattessich, Ph.D., is executive director of Wilder Research, which dedicates itself to improving the lives of individuals, families, and communities through applied research. Wilder Research has a staff of approximately seventy-five people, including evaluation researchers, survey interviewers, data analysts, administrative support staff, and others. Mattessich has been involved in applied social research since 1973, working with local, national, and international organizations. During the year that he prepared most of the manuscript for this book, he spent ten months in Belfast, Northern Ireland, where he learned from and consulted with organizations addressing youth development, community development, and the promotion and acceptance of diversity among groups from divided communities. Mattessich has authored or coauthored more than two hundred publications and reports, including the recently released second edition of the popular book *Collaboration: What Makes It Work*. He received his Ph.D. in sociology from the University of Minnesota.

Contents

List of Figures and Tables

Acknowledgments

This work has benefited greatly from the support, encouragement, and contributed wisdom of many colleagues and friends over the years. Tom Kingston and the board of directors of the Wilder Foundation kindly allowed me to spend a year in Belfast, Northern Ireland, where I devoted about half of my time to working on projects from the United States and the other half to working with organizations in Northern Ireland and completing writing projects such as this book. Without that year abroad, this publication might never have progressed from outline to final product. The David and Lucile Packard Foundation provided financial support as part of its initiative to improve the effectiveness of nonprofit organizations.

Within Wilder Research Center, I've learned evaluation theory and practice from Dan Mueller, Rick Chase, Greg Owen, Cheryl Hosley, and others. These individuals live every day within the exciting and fulfilling world of applied research. They accomplish the difficult task of conducting research that meets high-quality standards yet at the same time addresses real-world problems and issues within complicated situations. They dedicate their talents to the completion of projects that improve the lives of individuals, families, and communities, and I admire them greatly for the inspiration and instruction that their efforts provide.

Although she probably does not realize it, Marilyn Conrad enriched this book by contributing to the development of materials used in lectures and seminars that have provided the basis for several of the chapters. Also probably unaware of her positive influence is Ginger Hope, from whom I have learned significantly about effective communication. Well aware of his influence, but nonetheless deserving of praise and appreciation, is Vince Hyman, an editor with high standards and a great personality, who brought this book to a more valuable level than I could have reached on my own.

We could not achieve as much as we do at Wilder without the willingness of Wilder's program managers to look reflectively at their activities and to seek to improve program outcomes by means of research. Claudia Dengler has pioneered the implementation of a service effectiveness model within operating programs. Fundamental to this is good evaluation. During the past ten or more years, I have learned about the distinct nuances of designing and carrying out research and evaluation in different types of programs through conversations with Rod Johnson, Mary Heiserman, Dave Mayer, and Leni Wilcox. Recently, Craig Binger has struggled with and shed light on means for communicating organizational indicators for strategic policy development and strategic monitoring.

Mike Patton, Don Compton, and Mike Baizerman have critiqued various portions of this book, as these portions were initially developed for training seminars. They have offered insights and intellectual challenges that have enabled me to increase my skills. During the time I was writing this book, Paul Smyth and Frank Murphy opened the door to enriching and challenging experiences of doing research in a contested society and within different cultural settings. This expanded my awareness of what it takes to do effective applied research and enabled me to increase the scope of this work.

Last but not least, during our year abroad, which included time working on this book, Tara Mattessich helped me maintain the perspective that formal programs, clear outcomes, and rational, impartial analysis can take us only so far to improve the human condition. Family, love, and relationships are really where things are at. My children, Kate, Molly, Annie, William, and John, make that evident day in and day out.

The fault for errors, problems, ambiguities lies only with me, not with anyone noted above!

Introduction

So you have an interest in evaluation and research.

Perhaps you have a leadership role in your organization.
You want to make sure that your organization reaches the people whom you have a mission to serve. You want to make sure that the staff you supervise use the best possible techniques—whatever research shows to be effective. You want to make sure that you and your staff learn over time from successes and failures and that you continuously improve what you are doing. You may hear calls from the general public and from funders for demonstration of visible "results," and you want to respond to those calls.

Perhaps you are someone who allocates resources or sets policy.
You want to make sure that the organizations you support are, in fact, accomplishing their missions—reaching the people in need, using the best techniques, learning by doing, and improving themselves over time. You want to make sure that results are communicated, so that people in as many organizations and communities as possible can learn from the experiences of their peers in other locations. And you want to make sure that nonprofit organizations are accountable for their outcomes and that they represent their accomplishments in a credible way.

So that makes program evaluation of interest to you. How should you proceed? What steps should you take to make sure you get a good evaluation—efficiently and economically—that will produce the benefits you want?

Those questions led to the development of this book.

What this book does

This book encourages you to think about evaluation as part of an ongoing cycle of planning and designing programs, implementing them, monitoring them, and improving them.

If you plan, manage, or make resource decisions related to human service, health, or education programs, this field guide offers you an overview of what you need to know about *program evaluation* (also often called *outcome evaluation*). The information in this guide answers many common questions program managers ask about program evaluation.

This guide provides a reference tool for individuals who need to get a good evaluation done but won't usually do it themselves. This group includes executive directors, program managers, foundation program officers, government contract officers, agency board members, and others—all of whom face the prospect of hiring a program evaluator or working with a current evaluator on a new project. This guide helps you understand the basics of evaluation so that you can get the answers you need to work more effectively. It provides practical guidelines for your role in setting up an evaluation and for establishing a relationship with a researcher who does program evaluation.

If you are a researcher, this guide can offer practical insight into structuring effective evaluations. It will help you think about how to build relationships with the people with whom you will collaborate.

If you are a student who plans to enter the human services or social policy field as either a practitioner or a researcher, this book can save you a lot of time understanding the dynamics of doing program evaluation and working with an evaluation researcher.

Organization of the book

Chapter 1 imparts a general understanding of program evaluation, its uses, and its benefits. It shows that good evaluation resembles good common-sense thinking.

Chapter 2 describes what kind of evaluation information you need in order to answer strategic management questions. Chapter 3 reviews the phases and major activities of the evaluation research process. Chapter 3 also clarifies what you will do and what the evaluator will do during an evaluation.

Chapter 4 covers the topics of staffing and cost. Chapter 5 suggests some ways you can think about providing solid evidence as to whether your program truly makes a difference. Finally, the conclusion provides a few final words of advice as you begin to implement what you've learned in this book.

How this book differs from other resources

Many evaluation books and manuals focus on issues important for professional evaluation researchers but not of relevance (at least in great detail) for you — the organization manager or decision maker. I have attempted to make this book to fill your specific needs. It does so in at least two major ways: by teaching you enough to manage an evaluation process, and by helping you understand how to manage the relationship between your organization and an evaluator.

First, this book offers you a management-level understanding of evaluation, with the assumption that you might do some of the work yourself but will probably contract with a consultant or have an evaluation person on staff who deals with the nitty-gritty technical details. With that in mind, I included information to help you to think about evaluation, be conversant with the basic concepts, and not be deterred by evaluation jargon, so that you can determine for your organization what you need from an evaluation, how you will get it, and who will do it for you. Perhaps the best analogy is that if this book were a training program that offered instruction in a foreign language, it would bring you to a level in the language at which you feel confident that you know what is going on, can express your needs to others, and can take control of situations. However, it would not qualify you for a job as a translator at the United Nations.

Second, this book deals thoroughly with issues related to hiring someone to do evaluation. You might bring an employee on to your staff, or you might contract with an individual or firm. To make the best selection, you need to understand the pros and cons of different types of evaluators, likely costs and other resource issues, and a process for effective advertising and hiring. In addition, if you work with a program evaluator, whether an outside consultant or your own employee (who is, in a sense, an internal consultant), you will do so most productively if you understand the respective roles of the evaluator and yourself. This book outlines those roles.

Have fun! (And reach your personal aspirations)

You do the work you do because you want to accomplish something of benefit to others—something that will better a group, a neighborhood, a larger population, even the world. It's fulfilling work, exciting work. It's the work that has kept me involved with nonprofit organizations and public organizations for decades. When it stops being fun, or if it no longer gives a sense of accomplishment, then it is time to move on to something else. In the meanwhile, let program evaluation be a tool that enhances your ability to reach your aspirations to do the fulfilling, socially responsible work you want to do!

What Is Program Evaluation?

All of us gather evaluation information and make evaluative choices every day. The common sense we bring to decisions that guide our behavior strongly resembles the scientific principles that underlie program evaluation.

Take for example a common situation: You live in a new location and want to find the shortest route to work. Let's suppose three possible routes exist: A, B, and C. How do you determine which is shortest?

Perhaps you would drive each one—probably several times—and record the length of your trips. That, you would most likely say, offers the soundest method. After driving each route several times and recording the amount of time each trip took, you could come to a good conclusion about the shortest route.

How does this example demonstrate that you are already doing program evaluation? Figure 1, page 2, portrays how several of the features of your decision making about the route to work resemble features of good program evaluation.

Figure 1. Best Route to Work

Your decision about the best route to work	Similarities to program evaluation
Did you simply identify one route and use it, assuming it was the shortest? No. You gathered information.	Program evaluation doesn't assume that a program is effective. It gathers information and often compares alternatives.
Did you ask a community leader or religious leader "what is the best route?" No.	Program evaluation doesn't draw its conclusions from "authority." It relies on objective information.
Did you drive each route (A, B, C) only once, or did you try each of them several times? You tried them several times, gathering a "sample" of data on each one. In this way, you made sure that unusual traffic flows or road conditions on one specific day didn't give you a false idea about the length of the trip on a specific route.	Program evaluation emphasizes gathering enough information from enough sources to be sure of your results.
Did you look at your watch to determine the length of the trip? Yes.	Program evaluation incorporates reliable measurement instruments—measures that people accept as valid.
Did you tally the readings for each route and average them to decide which was shortest? Yes.	Program evaluation incorporates the analysis of information, sometimes using complex statistics but most often just through reviewing and interpreting simple data.
Did you write a report, call your family and relatives to a training session, and deliver the findings to them? No. You're not that crazy! (However, you might tell family and neighbors if they planned to travel to the area of your work.)	Program evaluation does include a communications phase to make sure that the results reach all the people intended to receive them. In addition, evaluation results are often communicated to other people who can use them. Typically, communications include both written and oral reports.

As you can see, program evaluation strongly resembles a thinking process that all of us use every day. It formalizes that process and makes it live up to certain standards. It also has its own jargon. In this book, we'll discuss how evaluation builds on decision-making skills that you use every day and how it offers you tools that enhance your capacity to make decisions about programs. Along the way, you'll pick up some of the jargon you're likely to hear from an evaluator.

Evaluation Defined

What is program evaluation? A definition that we have used at Wilder Research borrows from the work of many evaluators:

> *Evaluation is a systematic process for an organization to obtain information on its activities, its impacts, and the effectiveness of its work, so that it can improve its activities and describe its accomplishments.*

Let's look at the key words in this definition.

Systematic. Evaluation must be designed carefully, in a way that makes it reliable, credible, and useful. This implies attention to definitions of important concepts (for example, services provided, persons served) as well as the selection of methods that adequately meet scientific standards.

Process. Evaluation is ongoing. It involves work within many or all parts of an organization over time, with the intention to document what the organization is doing, and to provide it with a tool to measure and understand its activities and outcomes over a period of time.

Information. Evaluation is based on data. It provides information. It does not make decisions.

Activities, impacts, effectiveness. Evaluation identifies what an organization does (*activities*, including who is served and what they receive), it identifies what results this produces (intended and unintended *impacts*), and it identifies the extent to which an organization achieves the specific outcomes it intended for the people whom the organization seeks to benefit (*effectiveness*).

So that. The ultimate goal of evaluation is the use of information, either to better serve people in need or to represent the organization to others.

Keep each of these features of evaluation in mind as we continue to discuss the topic in more specific detail.

Benefits of Evaluation

Program evaluation provides enormous benefits. An effective evaluation will help you *learn about your successes, share information with key audiences,* and *improve your services.*

Learn about your successes

Even as evaluation helps you establish that your program is successful, it helps you deepen your understanding. Through evaluation, you

- Find out what works. Evaluation can help you understand how well your program works overall and how well specific parts of the program work. You can measure the extent to which you reach your goals or objectives.

- Hear directly from clients about what they like and dislike. Evaluation enables you to learn how your clients feel about your organization and what they think it does for them.

- Identify unanticipated results. Evaluation can bring to light impacts of your organization that were neither intended nor expected. These might include effects of your services on your clients that go above and beyond what you planned. The impacts might also include effects of your services on other individuals, families, or communities.

- Document needs of clients. By systematically gathering, compiling, and reviewing information over time, you can develop a sound understanding of how the population you serve is changing: what issues, concerns, and needs they have, and how those are changing over the years.

Share information with key audiences

Evaluation also helps you with other aspects of program management. For example, evaluation information can help you

- Recruit and retain talented staff and volunteers. People like to feel part of something meaningful. They like to see results. Evaluation findings can demonstrate to staff and volunteers in your organization the impacts that you have. Such findings can create a sense of achievement that makes people want to join the organization and stay with it.

- Attract new participants. Consider the impression it makes on you to see evaluation findings for services you are considering. For example, satisfaction ratings among customers of a store or among clients of a health care facility, or performance ratings for a repair shop, or "on time" statistics for an airline. The ratings themselves provide useful information to you. Moreover, the very fact that some organizations go to the effort to measure their performance and inform you about it increases your esteem for them.

- Engage collaborators. In addition to attracting new participants, the fact that you evaluate your programs and communicate findings to others increases their desire to collaborate with you. They will be more likely to refer people to you for services, and they will be more likely to want to collaborate in joint efforts.

- Garner support for innovative efforts. Innovation implies risk. If you want to develop a new program, someone will have to dedicate resources to it. By doing so, they take risks (for example, a financial risk that they may lose money on an ineffective program, or a public relations risk that they may look silly if the new idea does not achieve all it sets out to do). By establishing evaluation for innovative efforts, you will ensure potential supporters that they will learn the results of whatever risks they took. Moreover, a good evaluation turns an innovative project into an experiment. Supporters then look good whether the program achieves its results or not, because they have transformed the innovation into a public experiment from which everyone can learn.

- Gain public recognition. Solid research findings establish publicly and credibly exactly what a program can do.

- Respond to the call from funders and the public for "outcome-based management." Since not enough resources currently exist to meet all the needs that society has, those who provide financial resources (such as foundations, taxpayers, corporate donors) have begun to demand that organizations demonstrate outcomes. Evaluation measures and reports outcomes and responds to this call.

Improve your services

Finally, evaluation helps you build on successes and correct problems. You can use program evaluation as you

- Manage and monitor implementation. Having evaluation findings during the early stages of a program enables you to see immediately how well you are reaching potential clients and delivering the intended services. You can make modifications early to increase your speed in reaching your goals.

- Monitor and increase service effectiveness. As a result of your evaluation, you will understand what works and what doesn't. Beyond that, you will understand whether your activities are more effective with some types of people than with others. With this information, you can adjust to provide more of what works well, and you can search for alternatives for what does not work well.

- Improve the allocation of resources. Related to the previous benefit, you can use evaluation findings in combination with financial information to direct more resources to effective activities and fewer resources to ineffective activities. You can also combine evaluation and financial data to calculate the cost/benefit of alternative ways of providing your services.

- Retain or increase funding. Having credible evaluation findings increases your stature in the eyes of funders. Programs that can show what they are doing and how it makes a difference in the lives of individuals, families, communities will, on average, find themselves in a stronger position for funding. (Some of our long-term evaluation clients have reported that they've won grants and contracts—despite heavy competition and shrinking resources—because they base their proposals to private and government funders on complete, accurate, and impartial evaluation findings.)

Evaluation as an Ongoing Process of Doing and Learning

The Greek word *praxis* connotes doing or action. The word sounds a bit like practice. Many of us say that we "practice" our profession. In addition, all of our work is "practice" in the sense that we learn from it and constantly strive to do better.

Say *praxis* out loud, and it also makes you think of *action*. That's a good concept too, because applied research and evaluation should be dedicated to action. All our efforts need to culminate in effective action.[1] Indeed, in our definition of evaluation, we emphasized the words *so that* because the goal of evaluation is action: the use of information to make progress in helping individuals, groups, and communities. Evaluation is a tool to help improve action by your organization. Most evaluators receive their motivation not from writing reports but from observing the results of their work being translated into action.

How does evaluation fit into the process of service design and delivery? How does it inform decisions and lead to action?

Think about how you make decisions about what kinds of programs you should develop, or what kinds of services or activities you should offer. What goes into that decision? When I pose this question to groups of managers from nonprofit organizations and government, they usually offer a range of responses stating that they make decisions based on things such as "what we learned about community needs," "what funders expect and will pay for," "what's known to be effective," "what we're used to," and "what other people are offering."

The following paragraphs categorize the types of influences that affect decision making among managers who are developing a new program. They describe each category and suggest whether and how these influences should actually play a role in your decision making.

---

[1] Someone once said to me that the word *praxis* sounds a bit like *pray*—something that she and her nonprofit organization colleagues often found the need to do, but that's another story.

Research findings

Research findings include knowledge acquired through studies of at least four types:

- Assessments of needs. This research identifies the service needs or demands among the populations you have an interest in serving.
- Inventories of services.
- Research related to human behavior (in the social sciences, for example).
- Research related to organizational behavior (also in the social sciences).

Research provides a general understanding of what services might be appropriate for the people with whom you want to work. It can also document who else is providing services and assist you in deciding what your specific focus might be. The greater the amount of solid research you have relevant to your needs, the better.

Program evaluation findings

Program evaluation findings include knowledge provided by studies that explored the effectiveness of programs, services, activities, or treatments that are identical or similar to those under consideration by you. Once you have done some evaluation, they of course include your findings.

In general, you will want to use as much of this information as possible. Program evaluation findings offer a detailed look at how your program (or a similar program) works.

Practice wisdom

Practice wisdom includes knowledge gained by the professionals within your organization and by their peers in other organizations. It comes from the experience of working with the population you want to serve.

The strength of practice wisdom comes from the details it provides that research and program evaluation cannot. The weakness comes from the incomplete, sometimes biased perspective that practitioners in a specific organization develop because they see only people and situations of limited types.

Valuable Partners: Practice Wisdom and Evaluation

Practice wisdom is the knowledge gained by and shared among professionals working in a specific field. Such wisdom is invaluable, and it is through such wisdom that many improvements are made. It provides a depth of view not available through evaluation.

But practice wisdom has an important weakness: the professionals in a given field often come to share the same biased perspective based on an incomplete picture. This is where the more objective information provided by evaluation can help program professionals and managers gain a broader perspective than that available to them through experience alone.

Here's an example. Wilder Research once conducted a survey of 150 staff who worked in organizations that served elderly people. We asked the staff to describe characteristics of the elderly population in general—not the people they served, but *all*

older people. The survey respondents greatly overestimated the percentage of people in the general population who had disabilities, lacked family support, and could not achieve activities of daily living. This overestimate was expectable, since these staff formed impressions based on their observations, and they primarily saw elderly people with greater disabilities. But their "practice wisdom" was incorrect, and it would be risky to design new programs for the broader elderly population based on this misperception. (Such misinformed program decisions are made fairly regularly, with predictably poor results.)

The observations of service providers can limit their vision regarding larger issues, new developments in the community, and the overall conditions of the environment. The lesson: program managers can use evaluation in partnership with practice wisdom to see past their own biases.

Other influences

Other influences include all the remaining information, opinions, and other miscellaneous inputs that can make a difference in final decisions about programming. Some examples are

- The fact that a donor provided funds for a specific program or building or activity.
- The fact that staff are trained and experienced in one procedure and not in another.
- Politics of various sorts.

These influences are not inherently bad. For example, if a donor gives funds for something determined through research and evaluation to be very effective, that's all to the good. If staff are trained and experienced in the best possible techniques, that's good as well. However, quite obviously, these influences should not constitute your primary decision-making criteria. You would not implement a program just because someone has funded it, if, for example, research shows that it cannot produce results.

Figure 2. Program Evaluation as Part of an Ongoing Cycle

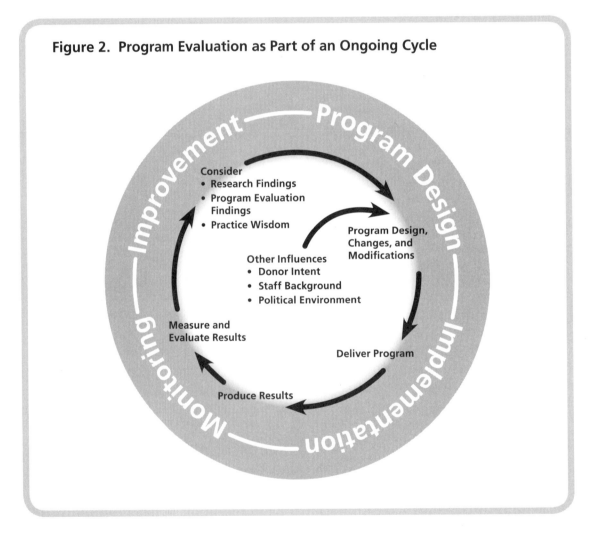

Figure 2 illustrates the ongoing cycle of program design, implementation, monitoring, and improvement among program managers and other decision makers. You use research knowledge, program evaluation findings, practice wisdom, and "other influences" to shape the design of a program. Then, you deliver or implement the program. This produces results. If you do evaluation, you can complete the cycle by measuring the results reliably and adding to your body of program evaluation findings. You can make program changes and continue repeating the cycle—all the time acting, learning, and improving what you do.

Summary

In this chapter, you have learned what evaluation is: essentially, the formalization of commonsense approaches to making decisions. You've learned about the benefits of evaluation and taken a first look at how you can use it in a process of ongoing improvement. In the next chapter, you will learn about the kinds of information you will need for an evaluation, and important questions you can answer with that information.

2

Evaluation Information:
What You Should Have, What It Will Offer You, and How a Good Theory Ties It All Together

"Not everything that counts can be counted,
and not everything that can be counted counts."
— Anonymous

"If you can define it, we can measure it!"
— Wilder Research

The first statement above is often mistakenly attributed to Albert Einstein. Whoever came up with it should be thanked by both applied researchers and human services practitioners. While not Einstein, the person did have a certain genius for "relativity," that is, the relative value of information.

The second statement comes from some friendly joking, which often occurs among the staff at Wilder Research and the programs with which we work. We remind our colleagues that although it sometimes appears that science lacks the necessary tools to measure what their program does, in reality that might not be the case. Rather, it might be that they need to work with us to clearly define their activities and goals. Once that is done, measurement procedures will be quite obvious.

Jointly, these statements usher us into this chapter with some important lessons to keep in mind.

- First, evaluation resembles other forms of research in its strengths and limitations. At any given time, it can do so much and no more. Just as in the world of physics, sometimes you suspect that something exists out there, but you can't quite define it, and your measurement tools can't quite detect it. Other times, your measurement tools have taken you as far as you want to go, and the next step is to come up with some new hunches or theories to lead you to further research.

- Second, for evaluation to serve you as a tool, you will need to be clear about what you hope to accomplish. You will need to develop formal definitions of words such as *service*, *activity*, *client*, and *outcomes*. You will need to state outcomes in clear terms.

In this chapter, we will spend time on two important topics: the types of evaluation information you need, and the development of a program theory for your program. Our discussion of types of evaluation information will enable you to recognize the information you need to collect in order to respond to important strategic and operational management questions.

The Value of Perception

Program managers often want to know what people think of the programs they offer. Some evaluators might argue that such perceptions of a program or service are not an "essential" type of information. In other words, one could in many cases demonstrate effectiveness without understanding whether people actually like a program. Strictly speaking, this is true. However, knowing how people feel about a program has many implications for planning and marketing the program. It also can offer valuable insight into why things work, whether they are likely to continue to work, and how they can be improved.

For example, few children will say they "welcome," "look forward to," or "have great satisfaction with" immunizations, even though such treatments protect them very effectively from serious diseases. If no one shows up for immunizations because the unpleasant experience outweighs the perceived benefits, the immunization program will be ineffective. This is a case in which measurement of perception is essential evaluation information; it's essential to change something in the program design so that parents will choose to immunize their children.

It lists four essential types of information and examples of specific elements they include (such as the age of the people in your program, their place of residence, their gender). As the word *essential* implies, you must have these four types of information to produce a high-quality evaluation.

The discussion of program theory will help you think about what you must do to "connect the dots"—to tie together the evaluation information elements you have into a portrait of how the services or activities of your program achieve their intended outcomes. Although a high-quality evaluation of some programs can occur without a program theory, the complexity of most programs makes the development of a program theory a requirement for a high-quality evaluation. In addition, many funders mandate the development of logic models (which are a technique for representing a program theory). In those cases, having a program theory becomes a requirement.

Types of Evaluation Information

To understand what your organization does and how effective it is, as well as to obtain ideas on how you might improve your services, your organization should, at a minimum, gather information of the following types, labeled *essential* and *additional*.

Essential information:

1. Participant/client information
2. Service data
3. Documentation of results or outcomes[2]
4. Perceptions about your services

Additional information:

5. Demographic information on the service area or market area that you serve
6. Data about needs in your community and other communities
7. Comparable measures from organizations similar to yours
8. Financial/cost information
9. Information that identifies the people you serve

---

[2] In our discussion, we reserve the words *results* and *outcomes* to refer to changes that occur because of the efforts by an organization among the persons, groups, communities, or organizations affected by those changes.

Essential evaluation information

You would be surprised at how many organizations don't collect and retain even the first two types of information listed on page 17. Many large, well-known, relatively effective organizations find themselves in the situation of having this information only partially.[3] It hampers their ability to evaluate their work and to improve their efforts as much as they would like to do so.

A description of the first four types of information listed and examples of them appear in Figure 3. Note that the examples are literally that: illustrations of typical elements of data that fall into a specific category and that many organizations collect. The specific information elements that you collect will depend on your needs and aspirations for the evaluation, your program goals, your program theory (which we discuss later), and specific hypotheses or questions that you and others have about effectiveness, accessibility, and why things work or don't work. These goals are tempered by practical considerations, such as what is reasonable to collect and what costs are involved. In any case, do not feel that you must gather all the information listed under "typical elements" in order to do a good evaluation.

If you have the information listed in Figure 3, you will possess the basic building blocks to represent your organization's efforts and accomplishments. By itself, the information listed there can enable you to respond to a large number of important questions you have. In addition, as new questions arise, you can organize the information in new ways to respond to those questions.

---

[3] See Paul W. Mattessich, "Lessons Learned: What These Seven Studies Teach Us," *Cancer Practice* 9 (2001): 78–84.

Figure 3. Four Essential Types of Information

Types of evaluation information	Examples of typical elements*
1. *Participant/client information.* That is, information on whom you serve, their characteristics, needs, and other attributes.	• Age, gender, ethnicity, income, education, place of residence, marital status, family status • Interests • Personal abilities • Needs, goals, problems to resolve • Capacities, resources
2. *Service data.* That is, type, volume, and other features of the services you provide or the activities you offer.	• Type of service or activity provided • Measure of service unit (a "session," an "hour," an "item," an "event") • Staff who offered the service activity (position, demographics, tenure, or other characteristics)
3. *Documentation of results or outcomes.* That is, evidence of changes that have occurred, accomplishments that have been achieved, needs that have been met among the people, families, groups, communities, or organizations that you serve.	• Knowledge gained, skills acquired • Problems resolved, needs met • Changes in the status of an individual, family, organization, community, or other group. (Changes can occur, for example, in behaviors, physical attributes, feelings, or relationships and patterns of interaction.)
4. *Perceptions about your services.* That is, an indication of how people feel about what you do in general, and about specific aspects of your activities. (Typically this information comes from users or recipients of your services, but it could also come from non-users.)	• Feelings about the organization overall • Ratings of quality of service • Ratings of staff performance (for example, their ability to do their job, to listen and respond to questions) • Ratings of facilities (for example, location, safety, ease of entry, appropriateness of furnishings and decoration for different groups) • Perceptions of accessibility (for example, hours, transportation, and other facilitators and barriers to use)

* As we stated earlier, you don't need to collect all of these. They are just examples.

Additional evaluation information

To accomplish the objectives you have for evaluating your organization, you may need the additional information listed earlier, such as the following:

5. Demographic information on the service area or market area that you serve
6. Data about needs in your community and other communities (for example, poverty rates, school achievement rates, illness incidence or prevalence rates, crime rates, or other social indicators)
7. Comparable measures from organizations similar to yours
8. Financial/cost information
9. Information that identifies the people you serve

We will discuss in the next section why this additional information is important when we look at the types of questions that evaluation information can answer. You can do a good evaluation without this extra information, but you will require it for some questions that you might wish to answer now or in the future.

Some people might argue that to truly demonstrate effectiveness, comparative data of some sort must enter into an evaluation; that is, comparative data are "essential," not "additional." This argument has some merit. In fact, later on we discuss the value of providing comparative data for increasing the credibility and usefulness of your evaluation findings. Nonetheless, a program just initiating evaluation can learn a great deal about itself without comparative data, and that program should not be discouraged if it can't obtain such data immediately. Likewise, some might suggest the necessity of cost data. However, an organization needs that information only if they want to study cost benefit or cost effectiveness.

Before exploring items 5 through 8, let's take a moment to discuss item 9, information that identifies the people you serve.

Information that identifies the people you serve

One special type of participant/client information is information that specifically identifies people whom you serve, that is, their names, addresses, Social Security numbers, phone numbers, and other details that can reveal their identity. Some of this you may gather as part of normal record keeping for your organization. Some of it may sit in a database that you use for recording membership, mailing information to people, or other purposes. Some of this information you may need to collect to determine eligibility to receive your organization's services. What about its use in program evaluation?

Information that identifies people individually *never* appears in the final report from an evaluation, but it often constitutes an absolutely essential element for the completion of an evaluation study. For example:

- You will need to retain an accurate record of names, addresses, and phone numbers if you want to do a follow-up survey of people who used your services in the past (for example, mailing them a questionnaire shortly after they used your services, or calling them for an interview a year after they used them).

- You may need to obtain addresses, if you don't already, for an analysis that will identify the places from which you draw people to your organization. (The evaluation jargon for this is *geocode*.)

So, you will generally need information that identifies people who use your services or take part in your activities in order to carry out a program evaluation, but it will not become part of the data that go into your findings.

Of course, some evaluation studies, especially those that only assess satisfaction at the time of an event or service episode and for which you have very limited expectations, do not require any information that identifies respondents. For example, a brief survey of persons who attended a presentation or an exhibit could occur completely anonymously. However, you could not return to those participants to assess their satisfaction at a later date or to determine whether they had been able to put to use anything that they learned at the session.

Questions Evaluation Information Can Answer

If you have the information we discussed in the previous sections, it enables you to respond to a number of important management questions, as Figure 4 indicates. For example, you can combine the essential information you've collected about your clients' characteristics with demographic information about your service area to answer the questions, "What proportion of our service area do we reach? Do we seem to reach certain types of people more than others?"

Figure 4, pages 22–25, can assist you in several ways. If you are designing an evaluation:

- The figure tells you what certain types of information can do for you.
- It offers a rationale for collecting certain information. You may need this rationale to justify an expenditure of time or money to collect certain information.
- It suggests evaluation questions for you to include in your design.
- It helps you communicate with a consultant about what you want and why you want it.

If you already have some information about your organization, the people you serve, and the services you provide:

- The figure suggests questions that you may want to consider asking.
- It enables you to determine, by means of the rows and columns, the questions that can be answered with the information currently at your disposal, either by itself or in combination with other information.

With the information from Figure 4 in your possession, you can make solid statements in response to important management questions. For example,

- By tallying the persons your organization serves, you can answer the question, How many people do we serve?
- By surveying people who used your organization's services, you can answer the question, How satisfied are people with our services?

- By collecting information about what happens to program participants after they leave, you can find out whether they accomplished what you hoped they would accomplish (for example, they found a job or pursued more education).

However, from your experience you probably know that organizations often want to do more than answer questions in isolation. Staff, boards, funders, and others often want to tie information together. They want to understand how an organization's activities lead to the outcomes the organization wants to achieve. To this end, a program theory provides a useful tool.

For the remainder of this chapter, we will discuss program theories and then illustrate a way to represent them (logic models).

Program Theories

Descriptive information tells *what* your program does and achieves. A program theory provides a coherent account of *how* and *why* your program generates the outcomes it produces (or is expected to produce). While you don't need a detailed program theory to do program evaluation, it certainly helps. Why is this so?

Imagine some simple situations requiring program evaluation:

1. You operate a program that brings children to a park on Saturday afternoons to play soccer. You have just two simple goals for the program: to bring thirty to fifty children from one neighborhood to the park, and to have the children report that they are happy with what they did and that they want to come back.

2. You provide kits to schools that enable them to offer art instruction to children in the sixth grade. Your only goal is to have the kits used.

Figure 4. Questions Evaluation Information Can Answer

Types of information	Questions you can answer with this information	Additional questions you can answer if you also have other information
Participant/ client informa- tion. That is, information on whom you serve, their characteristics, needs, and other attri- butes.	• What kinds of people do we serve? • How many do we serve? • What are their needs? • Where do they come from? • Are these the people we have the mission or intention to serve? • Have we reached the goals we have for num- bers and types of per- sons served? • Do certain types of people have needs that differ from those of other types of people? • Do we see certain pat- terns from year to year? • How are client charac- teristics, needs, or other attributes of the people we serve changing over time?	*With demographic information about your service area or market area, you can also answer:* • What proportion of our service/market area do we reach? • Do we seem to reach certain types of people more than others? • Do changes in the people we serve reflect changes in the service/market area? • What do the demographics and physi- cal location of the people we serve suggest about our accessibility? Do we seem more accessible to some groups than to others? • Can we predict likely changes in the area we serve that we need to plan how to address? *With cost information:* • What is our cost per person? • Does cost differ for different types of people? *With information from similar programs:* • How do we compare to our peers in numbers and types of people served? • Are other organizations experienc- ing the same changes? If so, has this occurred during the same time period? *With information on comparable geographic areas:* • Are the changes we see in our area similar to those in other areas? • Can we predict from the experience of other areas things that we need to anticipate in our area to meet the population's needs?

The lists of questions in columns 2 and 3 provide examples. They are not exhaustive lists of the questions that can be answered by the information in column 1.

Figure 4. Questions Evaluation Information Can Answer (continued)

Types of information	Questions you can answer with this information	Additional questions you can answer if you also have other information
Service data. That is, type, volume, and other features of the services you provide or the activities you offer.	• What services do people receive from our organization? Or what activities do they take part in? • How much do they receive or take part in? For how long? • Do certain types of people differ from others in what they receive, or in the amount, or in the length of time they use our organization? • Have we reached the goals we have for service? • How much service or activity do staff provide? What is the ratio of staff to service? • Do certain types of staff focus on or limit themselves to working with certain types of people we serve? • Do certain types of staff provide more or less service than others? • How do characteristics of staff match characteristics of the people we serve? • How is service data changing over time?	*With demographic information about your service area or market area, you can also answer:* • How do service area characteristics relate to the services or activities we actually deliver? • Can we predict likely changes in the area we serve that we need to plan how to address? *With cost information:* • What is our cost per unit of service, per staff person? • Does cost per service unit differ for different types of people who receive our services, or for different types of staff? *With information from similar programs:* • How do we compare to our peers with respect to service type and volume? How do we compare on costs? • Are other organizations experiencing the same changes as we? If so, has this occurred during the same time period? *With information on comparable geographic areas:* • Are the changes we see in our area similar to or different from those in other areas? • Do service delivery trends in other areas have implications for the way we should think about providing service?

Figure 4. Questions Evaluation Information Can Answer (continued)

Types of information	Questions you can answer with this information	Additional questions you can answer if you also have other information
Documentation of results or outcomes. That is, evidence of changes that have occurred, accomplishments that have been achieved, needs that have been met among the people, organization, or communities that you serve.	• Do we meet the needs that people bring us? • What impacts do we have on the people we serve, or on organizations or communities? • Have we reached the goals we have for effectiveness? • How have our results been changing over time?	*With demographic information about your service area or market area, you can also answer:* • Does anything special exist in our area that might enhance or limit how effective we can be? • Do the characteristics of those with whom we are effective match the characteristics of the people we most want to reach in our area? *With cost information:* • What does it cost to produce a successful "result"? • Does this differ for different types of people who receive our services, or for different types of staff, or for different regions of our service area? *With information from similar programs:* • How do we compare to our peers with respect to successful results or outcomes? • Do other organizations have the same experiences we do? If so, has this occurred during the same time period? *With information on comparable geographic areas:* • Do similar organizations in other areas produce similar results or outcomes? What are the implications of this for us?

The lists of questions in columns 2 and 3 provide examples. They are not exhaustive lists of the questions that can be answered by the information in column 1.

Figure 4. Questions Evaluation Information Can Answer (continued)

Types of information	Questions you can answer with this information	Additional questions you can answer if you also have other information
Perceptions about your services. That is, an indication of how people feel about what you do in general, and about specific aspects of your activities. (Typically this information comes from users or recipients of your services, but it could also come from non-users.)	• How satisfied overall are people with what they receive from us? • How satisfied are people with specific aspects of our service? For example, how satisfied are they with the friendliness and understanding of our staff, with our facilities, or with our hours of operation? • What suggestions do people have for improvement? • What seems to help people to access our services? • What seems to hinder people's access to our services? • Are certain types of people more satisfied than are other types of people (in general or with specific aspects of our activities)? • Have we reached the goals we have for how people feel about us and our services? • How are perceptions about our services changing over time?	*With demographic information about your service area or market area, you can also answer:* • Does anything special exist in our area that might enhance or limit satisfaction with our services? • Do the characteristics of those who are most satisfied match the characteristics of the people we most want to reach in our area? *With cost information:* • How do costs relate to satisfaction? *With information from similar programs:* • How do we compare to our peers with respect to satisfaction among people who receive service? • Do other organizations have the same experiences we do? If so, has this occurred during the same time period? *With information on comparable geographic areas:* • Do similar organizations in other areas report similar levels of satisfaction among people they serve? What are the implications of this for us?

Or, imagine these situations, which are slightly more complex and involve cause and effect:

3. Due to concern about the amount of street crime in a section of your neighborhood, you organize a neighborhood walking program in which volunteers agree to take turns walking in pairs every evening to watch for and report suspicious activity. You know the average daily incidence of street crime, and you want to see it decline as a result of your program's "patrols."

4. Some older people in an apartment complex have reported feeling lonely. You organize a program in which teenagers visit the older people. You hope that these visits will reduce reports of loneliness among the residents, and increase the knowledge of young people about the elderly.

In situations (1) and (2), you have clear goals and straightforward ways of meeting them. (Whether you *should* have more goals or different goals is another question.) The evaluator will assume that you know what you are doing, and that it's fine to run these programs to meet these goals. What is there to theorize about? Not much. You can meet your evaluation needs thoroughly by collecting and analyzing descriptive information, for example, how many children you bring to the park, how happy they are, and whether the art kits get used.

In situations (3) and (4), you acted on the basis of expecting that "A causes B." That is, you expected that people noticeably walking the streets in pairs will reduce street crime; you expected that visits by teens to older people will reduce feelings of loneliness and increase young people's knowledge of the elderly. These are simple causal theories. They begin to explain "why" something happened and can be used to make predictions of what might happen.

Your *program theories* in situations (3) and (4) are straightforward:

- "Why will (or why did) crime go down?" "Because of the patrols of walkers."
- "Why will people feel less lonely?" "Because they receive visits."

A program theory is a powerful management tool. Consider a well-known distinction made by Claude Lévi-Strauss, a famous anthropologist, who described the difference between the *bricoleur* and the *engineer*:[4]

- The *bricoleur* can use whatever is at hand to meet a particular need, without being able to explain why it works.

- The *engineer* develops and applies a theory to specific situations. The engineer understands why something works, can communicate that to others, and can use the knowledge gained from the theory to tackle new and related problems.

Like the engineer, a program manager with a program theory has more options and can act more productively than the program manager who engages in work without clearly stating (and then testing) how and why the accomplishment of that work actually results in the desired changes. A program theory enables you to:

- Tie all your evaluation information together in the most meaningful way.
- Understand why something works (not just see whether it works).
- Apply your knowledge to new situations.
- Combine your knowledge with the knowledge of others to produce more valuable and powerful information.
- Understand what additional information you need to gather and what you can omit. (It lets you know "what counts and what needs to be counted.")

All of this, of course, enables you to improve your programs over time and to do a better job fulfilling the mission of your organization.[5]

---

[4] See Claude Lévi-Strauss, *The Savage Mind* (Chicago: University of Chicago Press, 1966).

[5] For a good, brief discussion of program theories and evaluation, see Patricia J. Rogers, Anthony Petrosino, Tracy A. Huebner, and Timothy A. Hacsi, "Program Theory Evaluation: Practice, Promise, and Problems" in *Program Theory in Evaluation: Challenges and Opportunities,* edited by Patricia J. Rogers, Timothy A. Hacsi, Anthony Petrosino, and Tracy A. Huebner, 5–13 (San Francisco: Jossey-Bass, 2000).

A way to represent program theories: Logic models

Logic models offer a method to portray your program's theory. One format for logic models that has become popular during the past few years includes four major components: inputs, activities, outputs, and outcomes. Outcomes are sometimes subdivided into initial, intermediate, and longer-term.[6] Figure 5 shows what such a model looks like.

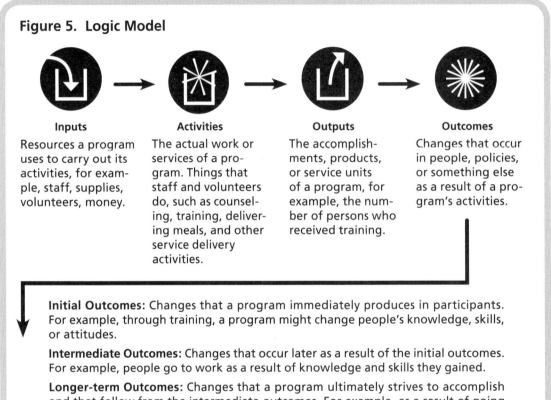

Figure 5. Logic Model

Inputs
Resources a program uses to carry out its activities, for example, staff, supplies, volunteers, money.

Activities
The actual work or services of a program. Things that staff and volunteers do, such as counseling, training, delivering meals, and other service delivery activities.

Outputs
The accomplishments, products, or service units of a program, for example, the number of persons who received training.

Outcomes
Changes that occur in people, policies, or something else as a result of a program's activities.

Initial Outcomes: Changes that a program immediately produces in participants. For example, through training, a program might change people's knowledge, skills, or attitudes.

Intermediate Outcomes: Changes that occur later as a result of the initial outcomes. For example, people go to work as a result of knowledge and skills they gained.

Longer-term Outcomes: Changes that a program ultimately strives to accomplish and that follow from the intermediate outcomes. For example, as a result of going to work, people maintain a stable income and reside in decent housing.

---

[6] See United Way of America, *Measuring Program Outcomes: A Practical Approach* (Alexandria, VA: United Way of America, 1996). Other formats for logic models and other ways to represent program theories have appeared over the years. They all constitute variants on a common theme in which a graphic, usually boxes and arrows, portrays a series of steps leading from what a program does to what the program is expected to accomplish. The different formats often use different terms to refer to the same concepts. Since the United Way's format has become popular, and because most program managers find it relatively easy to use, we include it here.

Figure 6 provides examples of two logic models: one for a teen smoking reduction program, the other for a job skills program. You may want to look at them to assist you in developing a logic model for your program.

Note that you do not have to gather information about everything that appears in the logic model. However, the model can alert you to information that is important to obtain in order to understand the effectiveness of your work.

Figure 6. Sample Logic Models

Logic Model: *Teen Smoking Reduction Program*

Program theory: Information and sustained support can enable teenaged persons to stop smoking. By providing a seminar and matching teens with a trained mentor, the program will change teen smoking behavior, with long-term positive consequences.

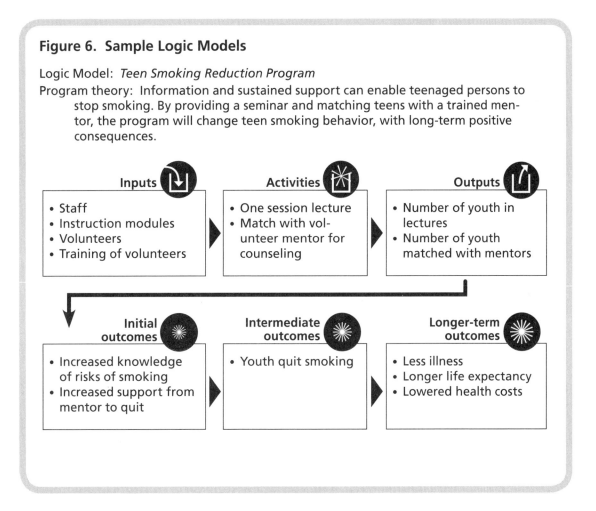

Figure 6. Sample Logic Models (continued)

Logic Model: *Job Skills for Unemployed Adults*
Program theory: Proper work attitudes along with good job skills and a supervised
  placement will lead to stable employment and reduction of welfare use.

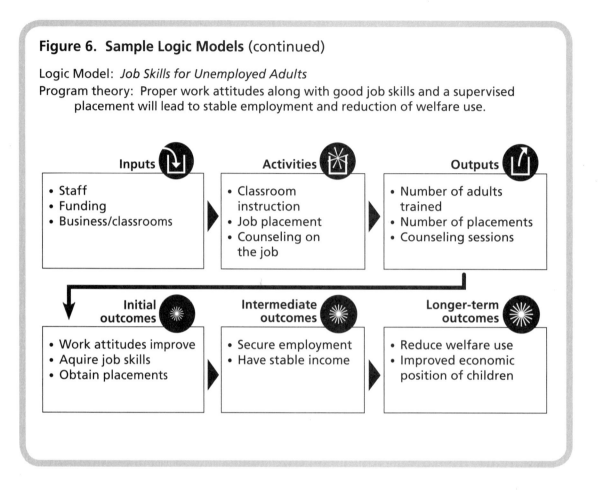

Now that we have discussed program theories and have seen a format for representing them, let's return to the assertion that program theories transform us into engineers who can understand why something works, communicate that to others, and use the knowledge gained from the theory to tackle new and related problems. Reflect on each of these in turn:

Understanding why something works

Consider the case of the job skills program in Figure 6. The theory represented by the logic model expresses how a set of three activities (classroom instruction, job placement, and counseling) leads ultimately to a significant social change (reduction of welfare use). This might seem trivial, but it is certainly not. To illustrate why, imagine two communities, each of which separately initiates a job skills program. The only difference between the two is that Community A has no program theory, while Community B does have a program theory.

In both communities, the number of people on welfare declines only very slightly after the first year of program operation. Due to the expense of the program, public officials and the public at large have become skeptical and demand that either outcomes improve or the program be discontinued.

Community A, without a program theory — thus without any understanding of the dynamics of reducing welfare dependency through job skills training — has no options other than to stay the course or to stop the program (and either do nothing or try a different program). If you disagree with this, try to explain what else Community A can do without using terms similar to those in the boxes labeled Outputs, Initial Outcomes, and Intermediate Outcomes.

Community B, on the other hand, has more options. For instance, it can reflect on the Initial Outcomes section of its program theory and measure how well program participants did on improving work attitudes, acquiring job skills, and obtaining placements. Assume that Community B discovers that participants who accomplish all three leave welfare, whereas those who do only one or two do not leave welfare. Community B can then change its activities to increase the likelihood that participants will accomplish all three Initial Outcomes.

The reason why Community B could take steps to improve it effectiveness, while Community A could not, is that Community B had something — a program theory — that enabled it to understand how and why the job skills program leads to the intended outcomes.

Communicate to others

Logic models are visual and communicate quickly. Note how easily and succinctly the teen smoking and job skills program logic models informed you of what the program does, what it ultimately hopes to accomplish, and everything that logically occurs in between. In the previous example, think how many more tools Community B's program will have to defend itself against cutbacks, while Community A's program is virtually defenseless.

Use the knowledge gained from the theory to tackle new and related problems

Consider the teen smoking reduction program in Figure 6. Based on the program theory, one can ask whether a program that increases knowledge and provides ongoing support might help in addressing other problems. For example, perhaps the same type of activities would help reduce drug or alcohol abuse among teens or other age groups.

Summary

This chapter has described the essential information you need for an evaluation of a program as well as other information that can help to provide a portrait of what a program accomplishes. It indicated how you can use different types of information, alone or in combination, to respond to important management questions for your organization. Finally, it discussed the value of having a program theory to tie together information about your program and to empower you to make wise modifications, improve your effectiveness, and apply your knowledge to a wider array of important issues.

Your next question might be, "OK. So, how do we do what needs to be done?" Therefore, in the next chapter, we will discuss the steps taken to design and implement a program evaluation, highlighting your roles and those of the evaluation researcher.

3

Phases of an Evaluation Study

All research studies, including program evaluation studies, go through the following phases:

- Design
- Data collection
- Analysis
- Reporting

In this chapter, we will discuss these phases and point to the important details of "who does what" in each phase. The chapter identifies your roles and the researcher's roles. The researcher (or evaluator) is the person who carries out the technical parts of the evaluation study. The researcher can be a consultant you hire, someone on your staff, or you.

No matter who does the work, you will want to assess whether the evaluator has designed a thorough study; to recognize, anticipate, and discuss potential costs; and to think about the roles of you and your staff in addition to those of the evaluator. Therefore, this chapter offers an overview of the four phases of a study and information about what happens in each phase.

Figure 7, page 34, describes the major steps associated with each phase of an evaluation research study.

In this chapter, we discuss the roles of the researcher and your roles related to each of the steps listed in Figure 7. (If you plan to do the evaluation research yourself, then the "roles of the researcher" listed in this chapter will also be your roles.)

Figure 7. Program Evaluation Phases and Steps

Phase of study	Steps in each phase*
Design	1. State the study goals, major research questions, and other major expectations.
	2. Specify your program mission and goals, and a program theory, as appropriate.
	3. Select appropriate methods.
	4. Finalize estimates of costs, agreements on roles, and plans for activities.
	5. Finalize and pretest methods.
	6. Train staff (as appropriate) and implement evaluation.
Data collection	1. Obtain necessary information using methods developed during design phase.
	2. Clean data.
	3. Compile and store data.
Analysis	1. Conduct statistical processing.
	2. Present and discuss preliminary analysis.
Reporting	1. Present findings to intended audiences.
	2. Make other presentations.

* Use of the word *steps* may imply a linear, sequential process. However, the process is not always linear. Sometimes, after reaching a particular step, a project may move back a step or two, based on new learning or a change in thinking. Also, if you do ongoing evaluation of your program, that is, if you gather information continuously and indefinitely in order to improve your work, then you will repeat the cycle of steps on a regular basis.

Design Phase

The adage from the strategic planning literature that "failure to plan is planning to fail" applies with equal weight to the field of evaluation. The design phase, in my opinion, is the single most important stage in your work. Decisions in this phase affect all later steps. Mistakes in this phase may limit, even completely eliminate, your ability to produce useful evaluation findings.

Sadly, many people, even professional evaluators, do not devote adequate attention to this phase. They suffer the consequences.

There are six steps within the design phase:

Design Step 1: State the study goals, major research questions, and other major expectations.

Design Step 2: Specify your program mission and goals, and a program theory, as appropriate.

Design Step 3: Select appropriate methods.

Design Step 4: Finalize estimates of costs, agreements on roles, and plans for activities.

Design Step 5: Finalize and pretest methods.

Design Step 6: Train staff (as appropriate) and implement evaluation.

You should understand what these steps accomplish and why you need to take them. Then, you can work with an evaluation researcher to structure your own approach.

State the study goals, major research questions, and other major expectations

Design
🔄 Step 1

In this step, you determine in general what you want the evaluation to do for you. Assuming that you want to measure whether the program accomplishes the goals it has, you will need to state those goals explicitly. For example, you might state goals such as:

• To enable unemployed people under age twenty-five to obtain stable employment.

- To improve the graduation rate within a school district.
- To increase the knowledge of children about contemporary painters and sculptors.
- To increase the amount of contact between older people and youth in the community.

You and the evaluator will likely discuss what these goals mean, and perhaps even revise them, until you feel comfortable that you have stated something in measurable terms that is worth measuring.

During this step, the specific questions that the evaluation will answer emerge from discussion among the intended audiences for the evaluation. For example:

- How many people do we serve in our program?
- With what percentage of people do we actually achieve our goals?
- Are we more successful with some types of people than we are with others?
- What do service recipients feel we need to do to improve?

It is important to pose questions appropriate for the maturity level of the program. For example, if your program is brand-new, and you know you will make many changes in it based on the first year or two of experience, you should probably frame most, even all, of your questions with respect to the program's activities and how they relate to the outputs (number of people who completed the program, for example). Wait until a later year to attempt to do a study of outcomes.[7]

---

[7] Some evaluation texts refer to this as the distinction between a *process evaluation* (looking at activities, services, staff, and organizational features of your operations to document the history and to see whether you deliver what you intend to deliver to the intended consumers) and an *outcome evaluation* (determining whether your program effectively produces the initial, intermediate, and longer-term impacts desired). Kristine L. Mida, *Program Outcome Evaluation* (Milwaukee, WI: Families International, 1996) discusses the problems that can result if you attempt to ask questions inappropriate for the program's level of development.

During this step, you also need to state other major expectations. These include:

- Expectations related to cost. You and the evaluation researcher will not reach final agreement on costs until Design Step 4. However, at the outset, you should indicate any expectations you have, for example, a "ballpark" range or a maximum budget (if one has been established).

- Expectations related to timing. If you feel that the evaluation should produce findings by a certain time, you should state that. If you have deadlines for making decisions, or if you do planning on a cycle that makes it desirable to receive information at a certain time of the year, you should inform the evaluator.

- Expectations concerning communication with the participants in your program. Some evaluation information comes from clients. Do you have expectations as to how or when clients can be asked to provide this information? Do you have expectations regarding what can or cannot be asked? Do you have expectations regarding confidentiality of information? If so, you should state these.

- Other expectations. You should state anything else you consider important regarding your preferences for the evaluation.

In this step, you do not make absolutely final decisions. Everything — goals, research questions, study methods, costs, and whatever else you consider important — is open for later negotiation and adjustment. However, you should strive to provide as firm an idea of your expectations as possible so that you, the evaluation researcher, your staff, and others do not expend effort only to be frustrated later when you realize that the work is not moving in an acceptable direction.

Roles of the researcher

- Work with you to identify intended audiences for and users of the evaluation findings.
- Lead a process that makes sure that the evaluation goals and specific questions are identified.

Your roles

- Identify intended users of the evaluation findings.
- Bring those users together, or set up a process that makes sure they have representation in the design. (This may include development of a "committee" of some sort to oversee the work.)
- Express your program goals, state questions you want the evaluation research to answer, and state any other expectations you have for the work.

How this step usually occurs

Some of this work often begins even before you have met with the evaluation researcher who will collaborate with you. For example, you might already have formulated your goals and the research questions you want answered. You may already have some general cost limits or some guidelines related to how you feel your program's clients or participants can be contacted.

However, much of the work occurs through interaction between you and the evaluator in meetings, written correspondence, and phone calls.

Most commonly, activities in this step include:

- Several meetings between you and the evaluator.
- A preliminary letter of understanding in which the evaluator states tentatively what the evaluation will accomplish, how it will occur, and what it will cost.
- A meeting of your advisory committee.

Design
Step 2 ➜

Specify your program mission and goals, and a program theory, as appropriate

This step is crucial whether or not you plan to do an evaluation now that measures the outcomes of your program.[8] Your immediate plan may just be to gather information about whom you are serving, what they receive from you, and how satisfied they are. However, eventually you will need to measure outcomes. Your initial evaluation should be designed with this possibility in mind.

---

[8] That is, an evaluation that gathers information of the third type, in the model we examined in the previous chapter (page 17).

Roles of the researcher

- Ask you to state your mission and goals in language that makes clear how you define effectiveness.
- Collaborate with you in development of a statement of your program theory.

Your roles

- Provide a mission statement and related information.
- State goals in clear, measurable terms.

How this step usually occurs

Most commonly, activities in this step include:

- One or more meetings between you and the evaluator. (These meetings, of course, may be the same meetings at which you accomplish the work of Design Step 1.)
- Review or drafting of statements of mission and goals, which you and other intended audiences for the evaluation modify and reach consensus about.
- Drafting of a logic model by you or the evaluation researcher for review, revision, and consensus among you and other intended audiences for the evaluation.

Select appropriate methods

Design
◐ Step 3

Whoever does the research should take the lead in this step. By now, he or she should have developed a good understanding of what you want to accomplish. Also, he or she should have reviewed and considered alternative approaches to evaluation that have been used for programs similar or identical to yours.

You will address the questions: What's the right method? How should we gather information? Remember that evaluation is just an extension of common sense. You know from common sense that no matter what you want to do—cure an illness, repair your car, have a pleasant vacation—a variety of methods exist. You will pick the one that best suits you at a particular time. You'll have certain priorities, and you will judge each option in terms of those priorities.

Similarly with evaluation, a variety of methods exist. Not all of them are right in all circumstances. In addition, some might fit at one point in the development of a program but not fit at another point. You and the evaluator will want to make sure that you match the method you use to the needs you have.

Warning: Be skeptical about any evaluator who jumps to a recommendation about research methods before fully understanding what you need to know and how you plan to use the findings of the evaluation research. For example, evaluators who talk "surveys" or "focus groups" too early in the conversation, or who emphasize that they always use "experimental design" or "qualitative methods," probably won't provide you the service you need. You have to identify what information you need, at what level of precision, and in what format and *then* work backwards to the appropriate method for obtaining that information.

Figure 8 shows a few typical methods for gathering information for an evaluation, along with examples of reasons why you and an evaluation researcher might select them.

Roles of the researcher

- Select methods of data collection that will meet the research goals.
- Draft a statement of methods that the evaluation will use. Discuss it with you, and revise it.
- Draft a statement that clarifies responsibilities for collection of information. Discuss it with you, and revise it.
- Instigate necessary research review and approval processes. These may include *human subjects review,* if required;[9] approvals or purchases of research instruments from license holders or vendors; and other approvals as needed.

---

[9] Most government-funded research and most research carried out by academic institutions must pass *human subjects review* prior to the collection of any study data (even for pretesting). A committee (the *human subjects committee*) must review the research design to assess informed consent, confidentiality, and risk to the participants in the research.

Figure 8. Typical Information-Gathering Methods

Method	Reason for use
Use of records	Commonly, forms completed by service recipients or staff, by phone or at a site, offer the best source of information on the demographics of service recipients, their reasons for applying to participate in the program or to receive a service, and other characteristics of service recipients that you will need for your evaluation. In addition, records documenting services received, attendance, or other activities will typically provide the information you require to understand the happenings in your program and who gets what.
Surveys: service recipients, persons associated with service recipients (for example, family members)	Telephone surveys, mail surveys, and in-person surveys offer a way to obtain information on what your program means for people and what effects it has. In most cases, service recipients themselves will participate. In some cases, family members might provide information. Surveys, if the samples are large enough and drawn properly, can provide sound information on how well the program achieves its goals, what perceptions people hold about the program, and other matters.
Focus groups: service recipients, staff, informants	Focus groups—groups of service recipients brought into meetings to discuss a program—can serve as a good means for obtaining information if you don't need a systematically drawn, large sample as the basis for drawing conclusions. Especially in the developmental stages of a program, focus groups can generate advice and suggestions for program improvement. Over time, they can play a similar role discussing issues and making recommendations. To some extent, you can learn about people's perceptions of the program. But the value of this information is greatly tempered by the lack of confidentiality, "group think" dynamics, and the unwillingness of some people who may have strong opinions to attend a focus group.
Observation by researcher	The measurement of some program achievements may require having a neutral party make observations, for example, to record behavior during a meeting or during a classroom instruction session.
Assessments by staff	Measurement of progress or outcomes for service recipients may sometimes require a professional assessment by someone acquainted with them. In this case, members of your staff may complete assessment forms.

Your roles

- React to the suggestions of the researcher. Give your opinions on the proposed methods.
- Accept tentatively or reject the researcher's suggestions for responsibilities for collection of information.
- Instigate any other review processes that your organization, its funders, regulators, and others in authority may require.

How this step usually occurs

- The researcher will probably spend time outside of meetings with you thinking about the best methods to respond to the study questions. The researcher will communicate with you about these methods via meetings, phone calls, and written correspondence.

- During the design phase, often at about this step, a good researcher will "fabricate" some findings and ask you, "If this is what you learned, would it enable you to do what you need to do?" Your response will either confirm that the design matches your needs, or it will indicate that the design requires adjustment.

Design
Step 4 ➜

Finalize estimates of costs, agreements on roles, and plans for activities

This step finalizes the overall design. After this step, everyone should be clear about what the evaluation will do, how it will be done, and what it will cost.

Note, however, that some projects move beyond this step and then back up to it. Several types of occurrences can produce the need to amend your "final" estimates of costs, agreement on roles, or plans for activities related to the evaluation. For example, the following situations will affect costs:

- Sometimes in finalizing your methods, you learn something that indicates you will need more time or more resources. Or you learn that a particular method will not work as planned, and you need to pick another method.

Sometimes you find out that information you assumed already existed actually does not exist.[10]

- Sometimes as the evaluation progresses, you identify additional needs for information. These require more time or other resources.

At about this point in the process, many programs find it helpful to develop a written document as a means of increasing efficiency and as a way to ensure that everyone understands their responsibilities. In a few pages, this document can lay out, for everyone's assent, the way the evaluation work will proceed. Figure 9, page 44, shows the typical contents of such a document.

Role of the researcher
- Prepare a final design, including adequate details about methods, responsibilities of all persons involved, and costs.

Your roles
- Ask challenging questions to make sure the researcher has developed the design in a way that will meet your needs.
- Review and come to agreement on the final details.
- Commit necessary resources.

How this step usually occurs
- This step should include a written statement to which everyone agrees.
- Activities during this step typically include meetings, phone conversations, mailed correspondence.
- The researcher may need to secure final agreements and final estimates of costs from others associated with the evaluation (for example, other organizations that are supplying information).
- Usually, the advisory committee (if you have one) meets to give their final "OK" to the work. This meeting can occur in person or via conference call.

---

[10] This happens frequently in organizations that have developed record systems to gather information, but have not made use of the information and have not maintained a quality-control process for the information. They typically learn that the database they assumed they could use actually has a severe lack of complete and accurate information.

Figure 9. Typical Evaluation Agreement

Outline section	Content
Name of the program	Whatever people normally call the program. If the focus of the evaluation is not the entire program, but some activities or services or project within the program, that can be named.
Overview of the program	A paragraph that describes what the program does, whom it serves, where it is located, and other key features of use that provide a context to someone who consults the document.
Activities or services provided	A list of the activities or services of the program, along with a brief notation of what each entails.
Program theory and logic model	A description and visual diagram, if possible, of how the inputs and activities of the program logically relate to outputs and intended outcomes.
List of program goals	A clear statement of each goal in simple, measurable terms.
Measurement or indicator for each goal	A description of the way that each goal will be measured. In many cases this can just be a reference to some items on a questionnaire, or to some information extracted from a form.
The procedures used to collect the information for each measurement or indicator	The "who, what, when, where." For each measurement, there should be a description of who gathers the information, using what instrument, at what time. For example, "A program assistant will complete the exit interview with each participant within the week prior to graduation."
Persons responsible	Anyone with responsibility for any part of the evaluation work should be identified, along with a list of his or her roles and duties.
List of data collection forms	All forms (program records, survey instruments, other) used for collection of information for the evaluation should be listed, and copies should be attached to the document.

Finalize and pretest methods

Design
◐ Step 5

This step brings you into the nitty-gritty work of the design phase. When you conclude this step, you will be ready to begin your evaluation. In this step, you and the researcher test measurement instruments (which you began to develop in Design Step 3), refine the instruments as needed, and develop forms that program staff will use to gather information.

As a consumer of evaluation information, you should satisfy yourself at this point that measures selected for the evaluation have the five characteristics shown in Figure 10 — relevance, validity, reliability, sensitivity, and timeliness.

Figure 10. Characteristics of Good Measures

Characteristic	Definition
Relevance	The measure is related to something important for your organization to know about.
Validity	The measure really measures what it is supposed to measure.
Reliability	The measure provides consistent, accurate "readings."
Sensitivity	The measure detects changes that you consider important.
Timeliness	The measure provides information in time to be useful.

Relevance

You assess relevance by looking critically at a measure proposed for your evaluation research to determine whether it appears to provide the information you need. Relevance is very much a common-sense judgment on your part: Will a measure result in information related to your needs? If you operate an in-home service program for the elderly, for example, a measure of older people's satisfaction with life might be interesting information, but it would not be relevant to your situation — unless your program has the goal to influence life satisfaction.

Validity

Validity (like reliability) comes from the statistical literature. A measure is valid if it truly measures what it appears to measure. So, for example, suppose your program hopes to change the attitudes of young people regarding other cultures, and let's say that you are elated to discover an existing measurement scale labeled "Attitudes toward Cultures Scale." That measurement instrument would seem to be relevant to your needs. Let's say that you happen to have a friend at a local academic institution who specializes in studies of cultural relations, and she knows everything there is to know about scales on this topic. If you ask her about it, and she states that research has demonstrated that this scale truly measures attitudes, then you are in luck. It's valid. On the other hand, you might have the misfortune to learn, for example, that research has shown that the scores on this scale really just reflect how much people know about other cultures, not what they feel. In this case, it would not be a valid measure of cultural attitudes.

Reliability

A reliable measure is one that provides a consistent rating, not susceptible to a great deal of error. So, for example, a reliable measurement tool will not provide a different result simply because measurements are taken at different times of day, or different days of the week, or by different staff who record the measurements.[11] A good example of a typically unreliable measure is asking staff who work in a program serving children and families to estimate, without tallying up records, how many of the program participants achieve certain goals. Such estimates suffer from the tendency of staff to give more weight to their recent, well-remembered experiences, rather than recalling what happened to the majority of families throughout the period of a year.

Sensitivity

Sensitivity refers to the ability of a measure to provide fine enough details. A measure that tells you only whether students complete a course or drop out, for example, might not contain enough information for you to take action. You might need to know more about their performance so you can identify ways to support them.

---

[11] Of course, some measurement instruments, such as clocks and calendars, should give different readings at different times, but that is another matter!

Timeliness

Timeliness is simply a practical issue. You may have certain deadlines by which you need information in order to make changes in your program. Therefore, an adequate measure needs to be able to produce results by that time.

Roles of the researcher

- Identify and obtain existing research measurement instruments, if they exist.[12]
- Design new research measurement instruments as needed.
- Develop guidelines and instructions for collection of information.
- Train all persons involved in the testing of measures.
- Revise and retest methods until satisfied with their productivity.

Your roles

- Review and comment on proposed methods.
- Inform staff of their responsibilities.
- Provide information related to a pretest sample.
- Provide necessary materials, space, and supplies in accordance with the plan.

How this step usually occurs

- Research staff work as much as possible on their own during this step.

- Your staff will be involved to whatever extent the design calls for their involvement. For example, your staff might assist in the selection of a sample and provide names of clients who will participate in surveys. They might contact people who will participate in surveys. They might organize records or collect information from existing records.[13]

---

[12] These may include survey questions that others have developed; they may include forms that you already have in place to collect information about the people you serve and what you do with them. Peter J. Pecora et al., *Evaluating Family-Based Services* (New York: Aldine De Gruyter, 1995), for example, describe instruments useful for measuring parental behavior and social support.

[13] To learn more about the activities associated with Design Steps 3, 4, 5, and 6, see "Practical Data Collection and Analysis Methods" in Leonard Bickman and Debra J. Rog, eds., *Handbook of Applied Social Research Methods* (Thousand Oaks, CA: Sage, 1998). It is thorough and provides more details than we can discuss here, yet is quite readable with a minimum of jargon.

Design
Step 6 ➡

Train staff and implement evaluation

This is the transition from practice to the real thing. It is the time when all systems are go and the countdown begins.

Roles of the researcher

- Train data collectors, as appropriate.
- Closely monitor implementation and make adjustments as needed.

Your roles

- Communicate, as necessary, about the evaluation with all appropriate parties. These may include staff in your organization, the people your organization serves, staff from other organizations that will be asked to participate in the evaluation in any way, and any others who need to know about the evaluation.
- Train your staff related to their responsibilities within the evaluation. (If the evaluation researcher will do this, then just facilitate the process as necessary.)

How this step usually occurs

- As in Design Step 5, research staff work as much as possible on their own during this step.
- Your staff will be involved to whatever extent the design calls for their involvement. For example, your staff might assist in the selection of a sample, and provide names of clients who will participate in surveys, contact people who will participate in the surveys, and organize records or collect information from existing records.

With Design Step 6 under way, the evaluation moves on to the data collection phase.

Data Collection Phase

Even in this age of sophisticated technology, the collection of data remains a very human, very personal process. Some person at some point in the process has to write something down or strike a keyboard. The potential for human error looms large. In the data collection phase of your work, you must attempt to ensure that whatever gets recorded represents "reality" as closely as possible.

Somebody might complete a questionnaire; two people (an interviewer and a respondent) might ask and answer questions; someone might tape-record and transcribe a meeting; someone might respond to questions on a computer. In each case, people think, people use their senses to see, hear, touch. People make judgments. People strive to tell the truth, and people sometimes try to paint an image of reality that differs from what really exists. People make mistakes.

We cannot improve the quality of data once those data have been collected. High-powered computers and complex statistical analysis cannot transform incorrect information into correct information. They cannot create data that nobody collected in the first place.[14]

The major lesson? During the data collection phase, you must emphasize the importance of gathering exactly what you need in a reliable, credible manner. If you don't, your study may have no value.

There are three steps within the data collection phase:

Data Collection Step 1: Obtain necessary information using methods developed during the design phase.

Data Collection Step 2: Clean data.

Data Collection Step 3: Compile and store data.

---

[14] This does not imply that we cannot do "estimates" to try to portray what's missing or to correct what's wrong. But that is another process, and one that is not as desirable as having the right information there from the start.

Data Collection
Step 1 ➔

Obtain necessary information using methods developed during the design phase[15]

This step is when people complete forms, take part in surveys, or do whatever other activities you need to obtain information.

Role of the researcher

- Collect information. In some cases, researchers will do this on their own; in other cases, they have assistants who gather the necessary information through interviews, mailed surveys, or whatever appropriate means.

Your roles

- Make your records available, as needed, to provide data already collected and contact information for people who will participate in the evaluation study.

- Your staff may gather and record information, by completing forms or doing assessments, for example.

How this step usually occurs

- Research staff conduct surveys, carry out focus groups, and review and tabulate information from records, as needed.

- Your staff is involved to the extent specified in the design.

Data Collection
Step 2 ➔

Clean data

This step involves checking and correcting information.

Roles of the researcher

- Research staff inspect data to make sure they are accurate.

- Research staff make corrections, as appropriate.

- Sometimes people who provided information or who responded to surveys receive a call to clarify an ambiguity or to provide data that were omitted.

---

[15] A readable, mildly technical description of major concepts and activities related to design, data collection, and analysis appears in Michael J. Smith, *Program Evaluation in the Human Services* (New York: Springer, 1990).

Your role
- Usually no effort on your part, other than occasionally to respond to questions the research staff might have for you.

How this step usually occurs
- Deep in the heart of data central, eccentric researchers work with the survey responses.

Compile and store data

Data Collection
G Step 3

In some way or another, the information you have gathered for your evaluation study has to make its way into a database. You will use this database as the source of your findings. Whether you put information into a computer or organize it on pages of paper, you need something that is coherent and that you can efficiently consult and analyze to draw conclusions.

Roles of the researcher
- Code data. If data collection involved "open-ended questions" or text, that information needs to be put into an analyzable form. Most typically this involves development of a coding system to categorize responses for later statistical tallying and analysis.
- Enter data into a data file for analysis, as appropriate. In most cases, this involves constructing a computerized data file. In limited cases, data may simply remain on paper for tabulation by hand.

Your role
- Usually no effort on your part.

How this step usually occurs
- Those eccentric researchers take care of it.
- Once data are compiled and stored, this phase has ended. It's time to analyze the data.

Analysis Phase

In this phase, you look at the information you have collected and determine its implications. There are two steps within the analysis phase:

Analysis Step 1: Conduct statistical processing.

Analysis Step 2: Present and discuss preliminary analysis.

Analysis
Step 1 ➔

Conduct statistical processing

Here, the evaluators tally findings, look at differences among groups, and try to determine how different bits of information relate to one another.

Roles of the researcher

- Develop descriptive statistics that summarize all the information gathered through the study.

- Perform statistical analysis as required to answer the study questions. This could include an examination of differences between different types of clients, or comparing findings on your program to other programs or benchmarks. As an example of the first case, the descriptive data may have shown you that, overall, 88 percent of the people you serve are satisfied, but you might want to know if satisfaction is greater among women than men, or greater among Jamaicans than Puerto Ricans. As an example of the second case (comparative findings), the researcher might bring census data into the analysis in some way. If your program addressed needs at a community level, the researcher might find other communities to compare with yours.

Your role

- Again, very little. You probably feel a bit lazy by now, and maybe you even forget what the researcher looks like, but remain vigilant. You play an important part in the next step.

How this step usually occurs

- The researcher analyzes information using appropriate statistical methods. In some cases, data can be tallied by hand. In most cases, computers will perform the analysis.

Present and discuss preliminary analysis

Analysis
Step 2

In taking this step, you will look at findings, discuss and critique them, and typically ask for more analysis until you feel you have answered all the questions you can answer. During this step, it is important to have an open mind, be inquisitive, and challenge findings from all points of view. In this way, you will produce the most creative and most credible product.

Roles of the researcher

- Bring drafts of findings to you and others for review.
- Provide preliminary interpretations and suggestions for action.
- Facilitate careful discussion of findings, interpretations, and suggestions for action.
- Listen to your comments, and return to Analysis Step 1 for additional statistical processing, as needed, to respond to your questions.

Your roles

- Carefully review findings.
- React to findings and give ideas for final report.

How this step usually occurs

- One or more meetings between you and the researcher.
- One or more meetings of the advisory committee.

Reporting Phase

In this phase, you share findings with the intended users of the information, as well as with others whom you consider appropriate. There are two steps:

Reporting Step 1: Present findings to intended audiences.

Reporting Step 2: Make other presentations as needed.

Reporting Step 1 ➋

Present findings to intended audiences

In this step, you and others receive the official findings. There should not be any surprises because you have already reviewed the preliminary findings. However, that does not mean you will like the findings. The researcher has done the job as an independent professional.

Roles of the researcher

- Produce a report that includes, at a minimum, a description of the findings of the evaluation research, an interpretation of the findings, suggestions for future action, and a description of the method used, including the strengths and limitations important to acknowledge in interpreting the findings.
- Present and discuss findings with you and other intended audiences.

Your roles

- Receive the report.
- Participate in discussions.
- Initiate steps to get the evaluation findings put to use for program improvement, policy influence, funding, or whatever uses are important.

How this step usually occurs

- Advisory committee meeting.
- Presentations to staff and others intended to receive the results.
- Production of a written report.

Reporting Step 2 ➋

Make other presentations as needed

The work done to evaluate your program may have relevance to others. You may feel that your program's research should have an influence on policy and practice within your field. If so, then you may want to share the findings locally and nationally with colleagues in similar organizations, funders, public officials, professional networks, academic institutions, and others.[16]

---

[16] Books have been written about the dissemination of research findings, how to go about it, and what influences the use of findings by program developers and policymakers. See, for example, chapters by Iwaniec, Pinkerton, and Kelly in *Making Research Work*, edited by Dorothy Iwaniec and John Pinkerton (Chichester, England: John Wiley & Sons, 1998); Paul W. Mattessich, Donald W. Compton, and Michael Baizerman, "Evaluation Use and the Collaborative Evaluation Fellows Project," *Cancer Practice* 9 (2001): 85-91; Valerie J. Caracelli and Hallie Preskill, *The Expanding Scope of Evaluation Use* (San Francisco: Jossey-Bass, 2000); and work that Wilder Research is currently developing on uses of evaluation studies.

Roles of the researcher

- Produce additional reports of study findings.
- Present findings at meetings and conferences.[17]

Your roles

- Identify audiences to whom you would like to address the findings.
- Set up meetings, presentations.
- Commit necessary funding for presentations and reports.
- Participate in presentations. (Do them yourself, if you like!)

How this step usually occurs

- A public report, and sometimes a press release, is written.
- Meetings are held with media representatives.
- Presentations are made at a special meeting or conference related to the findings.

Time-Limited Projects versus Ongoing Evaluation

The description of four research phases may appear to apply only to time-limited studies, such as a one-time program evaluation that will last about two years, report its findings, and not continue beyond that time.

However, the phases also apply to ongoing evaluation research, that is, evaluation that gathers and reports information indefinitely, as a constant resource for program improvement. In this case, the design phase repeats itself periodically as a review activity. The later phases continue uninterrupted, on schedule, subject to change only if the latest design work makes alterations of any type.

---

[17] The presentations and reports in this step of the work have a cost. If resources have not been built into the final agreement (during Design Step 4), they need to be committed before the work commences on these extra reports and presentations. However, such presentations can have important mission-related benefits (for example, to influence public policy, change standard practices, create positive public relations, or attract new funding).

Summary

The steps described in this chapter comprise the sequence of events through which all program evaluation passes in one way, shape, or form. The chapter has offered you an understanding of program evaluation activities and has alerted you to what you can typically expect at different phases of a program evaluation. The chapter identified certain roles as "yours" and certain roles as belonging to "the researcher."

Of course, you still need to decide what you might do on your own and what you might hire someone else to do. Therefore, in the next chapter we discuss the staffing of evaluation research, describe various options you might consider for consultants, and offer suggestions for making your relationship with an evaluation consultant as productive and satisfying as possible. We also look at other practical issues such as costs and contracting.

4

Staffing the Evaluation and Estimating Costs

"Should we hire someone, or do this on our own? Or both?"

No universal answer exists for this question. In honesty, it all depends on many factors. For example:

- What capability do you and your staff have to do the work?
- How complicated is the process of measuring what you need to measure?
- Are you starting from scratch, or does a system already exist that can provide much of the information you need?

As you would if you wanted to construct or repair a home, you have to make a decision based on your abilities and your priorities. Most people cannot design and build their own home, but some can. Many people can do minor repairs in their homes, but they call a plumber, electrician, or other professional for major work. Some people can do work that has all the necessary technical features, but if a repair job in a location highly visible to visitors requires both technical quality and good looks, they call a person with more experience who can do both.

Figure 11 lists some options and the circumstances that might lead you to select an option as the best for you.

Figure 11. Options for Staffing the Evaluation

Option	Considerations
Do the work completely on your own: design, data collection, analysis, and reporting. (No use of a consultant at all.)	• You have a research person on staff (or you are one yourself) for the necessary design and oversight. • You have the time and other resources to do the work. • You have staff who can assist, as needed, with collection, analysis, and reporting of information.
Hire a consultant for design only. Do the other work on your own: data collection; analysis; reporting. Then, hire a consultant occasionally for dealing with problems and advice on expansion or making changes.	• You and your staff don't have the necessary skills for the overall design, or at least for certain complex portions of the design. For example, you are not familiar with the necessary methods or data sources. • You and your staff don't have the time to design a new system. • You have staff who can implement and maintain a system, with a little advice and coaching from an expert, after the system has been designed.
Hire a consultant to handle all phases of the work.	• You lack the staff, the capability, the time, and other resources to do the work.

Some other considerations may motivate you to use a consultant. In a sense, these are trump cards. Whether or not you have the necessary experience, staff, time, and other resources to do the evaluation on your own, these circumstances take precedence:

- *The need for the objectivity and neutrality.* You may need to make sure that some or all of the primary audiences for your evaluation have confidence that the work was done by someone with no affiliation or vested interest in your organization and its programs.

- *Requirements of your funders.* Organizations that provide you with funds may require that you participate in an evaluation conducted by a third party. They may do this for purposes of objectivity, but they may also do it as one part of a larger effort to accumulate and combine common evaluation findings from multiple programs.

Note: Cost and available funds do not appear in these considerations, because it would be irresponsible to suggest that you should do the work on your own solely because you need to save money, or that you should hire a consultant just because you have some extra funds in your bank account. You first must decide which options can produce a quality product. After you have identified the options that can produce a quality product, you can then use cost, as well as other features, to help you make your final selection. If hiring a consultant is the only way that research of adequate quality can occur, but you don't have any money to do so, then you will need to either obtain the necessary funds through a grant, or not do the work at all.

Selecting a Research Consultant

Over the years, I have met many people from nonprofit organizations who felt let down by their experience with research consultants. These include:

- Someone whose organization was impressed by the comprehensiveness of a research proposal from a large, international accounting firm. They paid a great deal of money for the work, but in the end, they felt the final product did not meet their needs. The reasons for this failure to meet their needs, they suspected, were that the consultants had no experience working with small nonprofit organizations, and the specific model the consultants applied to the project had originated within a business school framework for use with for-profit organizations.

- Someone whose organization expected a group of university students to do an evaluation study as a class project "for free," only to learn to their dismay that the school semester did not allow enough time to do the work required. So, they ended up with only a literature review.

- Someone from an organization who hired an evaluator who promised a "thorough qualitative evaluation that will explore the program in depth." What they received was a set of good, narrative stories. This greatly disappointed their funders, who expected basic facts that indicated how many people participated in the program, how many completed it, which ones seemed to benefit from it, which ones didn't, and why.

What do these experiences teach us? They do *not* imply that large accounting firms, university students, or qualitative evaluators cannot do the kind of research you want them to do. In fact, they can all do excellent research under the right circumstances. Rather, in each of these examples, the organization that hired a research consultant did so for the wrong reasons.

So, the major lesson from these examples: Look carefully at the consulting vendors available to you and determine how well each of them can meet the needs you currently have. Regardless of how well or poorly various consultants have worked with you or others before, the question you should raise is: Does the consultant have the ability to work with us now and meet the needs we currently have? You need to match your specific needs with the capability of the consultant.

In the next few sections, we will discuss some general principles to keep in mind when selecting a consultant.

Types of vendors

It's hard to categorize and make generalizations about types of vendors—any attempt misrepresents some of the people placed in a category. Nevertheless, over the years, I have noticed certain traits that tend to distinguish one type of consultant from another. You need to understand these in order to make the best decision about the person and organization with whom you would like to work.

Independent professionals, working alone. This category includes freelance consultants, solo practitioners—people who operate on their own. They may have a small staff of clerical and research assistants. However, only a small proportion of them have employees who specialize in things such as statistical analysis, database management, and survey interviewing. In small projects, they tend to do all the work themselves; in larger, more complex projects, they subcontract with others for portions of the work. They may or may not limit themselves to working with nonprofit organizations.

Research/consulting organizations, not-for-profit. This category includes freestanding research organizations and research groups that are part of a larger organization, such as a service provider or a foundation. These organizations may have anywhere from a few research staff to several hundred. Almost always they have research support staff (research assistants, statistical analysts, database managers). Usually, they have the capacity to do surveys on their own (phone and mailed) up to a certain scale. Beyond that, they often subcontract or decline projects. These organizations often dedicate themselves only to program evaluation. Sometimes, they also limit the focus of their work to a specific topic. Sometimes, they do both evaluation and other forms of applied research (research intended to assist in the development of programs, policies, or other activities). Typically, they specialize in work with nonprofit organizations; if they work with for-profit organizations at all, they usually do so only for projects with a "public benefit." For example, such an organization might decline to do work for a bank if the proposed project focused on customer marketing issues. However, if the same bank approached it to do a study of a program intended to help low-income residents increase their resources in order to become home owners, then the organization might take on the project.

Research/consulting organizations, for-profit. This category includes organizations similar in characteristics to the not-for-profit research/consulting organizations. However, they usually do not specialize in work for nonprofit organizations and public benefit projects. In fact, they often emphasize work with for-profit clients and government agencies. For the larger firms, evaluation and other forms of applied research often constitute only a small proportion of their work.

Academic research centers/university faculty. This category includes academic centers that formally offer services, and faculty who work essentially independently but under the auspices of a university.[18] Such centers may include just a few faculty or virtually everyone in the university, depending on how they develop their membership and market their services. They also often have some graduate students who serve as research consultants. They typically have staff and students with various levels of experience and skills related to statistics, data processing, interviewing, and other research activities. They often have established relationships with a survey research center in their institution, for survey work.

Figure 12 lists these types of vendors and provides a general assessment of their positives and negatives. The figure can serve as a general guide to what to look for, what to be cautious about, and what to probe for as you talk to various research vendors. When you make your actual decision, however, you should consider each consulting option you have on its own merits. Obviously, in your decision making, you will want to blend the general features of vendors, in Figure 12, with specific information you have obtained about each of your candidates, for example, their experience, their reputation (if you can speak with some others about them), and the way they presented themselves when you interviewed them.

One other source to consider is evaluation resources on the world wide web. I did not list a separate category of "web vendors" because all the Internet sites that I have seen that provide evaluation resources are sites operated by individuals or groups in one of the four categories listed. These sites attempt to assist with evaluation in a variety of ways. Some simply provide samples of measurement instruments used in previous research. Some try to describe the evaluation process and offer "how to" lists. The more sophisticated ones offer interactive procedures for many of the steps that we discussed in Chapter 3.

At their present state of development, the web purveyors of evaluation services are of uneven quality. Some are not helpful at all and are potentially even harmful. Others have good content but are not particularly user-friendly.

---

[18] A university faculty member who does his or her work outside of the auspices of the university, essentially as a separate job, would fit more appropriately into the first category, "independent professionals, working alone."

Figure 12. Pros and Cons of Vendor Types

Type of vendor	Positives	Negatives
Independent professionals, working alone	• Can often offer more customized attention and more time than other vendors • May specialize in just your field	• May lack close access to specialists and peers for obtaining advice and sharing work • Not "full-service"; can't do all phases on their own • Sometimes can't do large projects
Research/consulting organizations, not-for-profit	• Nonprofit mission (understand nonprofit organization culture) • Often full-service capacity—can do all phases of work • Large number of staff, often including specialists and content experts	• Sometimes can't do "small" projects • Sometimes overworked, with inadequate resources
Research/consulting organizations, for-profit	• Often full-service capacity—can do all phases of work • Large number of staff, often including specialists and content experts	• Often not interested in working with nonprofit organizations • May be expensive • Sometimes can't do small projects
Academic research centers, university faculty	• Credibility of their institution strengthens the image of your work • Often full-service	• May be more interested in their agenda than yours (common complaint) • Not always full-service

As you would expect, some use their web sites as a marketing tool, to start a process that eventually brings people into a standard consulting relationship. This situation will probably improve over the next five years, and it will then be possible to make general statements about the pros and cons of using web sites as consultants or vendors of evaluation services. In the meanwhile, it never hurts to look around and obtain different perspectives and ideas, but don't delude yourself into thinking that web sites can equal the quality of personal interaction.

What Should You Look for in a Consultant?

Following are questions to ask (and characteristics to look for) as you interview evaluation consultants.

- Will the consultant tailor the process to fit your needs? Does he or she bring a cookie-cutter or "one size fits all" approach? Does the consultant ask questions that indicate flexibility in design?

- Does the consultant seek information about the larger context in which the evaluation project will occur?

- Does the consultant think strategically to understand the connections among the evaluation, your short- and long-term goals, and other issues your organization faces?

- Does the consultant seek to understand the variety of audiences whom the evaluation will serve? In what ways does he or she indicate an understanding of how the results can be used with various audiences and for various purposes?

- Does the consultant take a clear, practical, data-based approach?

- Does the consultant have experience commensurate with the project tasks, including familiarity with populations similar to those you serve and knowledge about issues the evaluation will likely face? Has the consultant worked with organizations similar to yours?

- Do you have a good rapport with and good feelings about the consultant?

- Is the consultant currently available, with the capacity to do the work when you need it done?

- Do you accept the consultant's work style?

- Are you confident about the impression this consultant (or assistants) will make when speaking with your clients, board, staff, funders, volunteers, or other important constituents?

Let the buyer beware

Evaluators come from many different backgrounds, a situation that the *American Journal of Evaluation* prizes (rightly or wrongly) and states as a guiding principle:

> American Journal of Evaluation *is based on the principle that the techniques and methods of evaluation transcend the boundaries of specific fields and that relevant contributions to these areas come from people representing many different positions, intellectual traditions, and interests.*

I do not defend that principle—I just state it for your consideration. In my opinion, the wise consumer, after reading it, should say, "let the buyer beware." This does not imply that incompetent and unscrupulous evaluation professionals prey upon unsuspecting people such as yourself. However, it does expressly state the official recognition that the title "evaluator" does not suggest a common base of skills, knowledge, or approaches to research design.

The field of accounting, in contrast, has established that all accountants subscribe to at least a minimal common set of concepts. New accountants are trained in those concepts; if someone has an accounting degree, the consumer knows that they received such training. A national Financial Accounting Standards Board rules on accounting standards, rules, practices, and methods with the force of law. No similar testing or credentialing mechanism has emerged within the evaluation profession.[19]

Finding an Evaluation Consultant

Three common methods for finding an evaluation consultant are word of mouth, contacting the state chapter of the American Evaluation Association, and advertising through a request for proposals (RFP). Each of these has its

---

[19] James W. Altschuld, "The Certification of Evaluators: Highlights from a Report Submitted to the Board of Directors of the American Evaluation Association," *American Journal of Evaluation* 20 (1999): 481-93; and Steven C. Jones and Blaine R. Worthen, "AEA Members' Opinions Concerning Evaluator Certification," *American Journal of Evaluation* 20 (1999): 495-506 outline the pros and cons of a certification process and reveal little consensus among professional evaluators concerning the need for such certification.

positive and negative features. They are not mutually exclusive; you might combine any or all of them. A brief discussion of these methods follows.

Word of mouth

You can always ask people you know in other organizations to identify evaluation consultants with whom they have worked. If your network is limited, contact people in your field and allied fields, introduce yourself, and ask whether they have used an evaluation consultant whom they can recommend. Ask how well the consultant performed and obtain at least a general understanding of the consultant's approach to see if it will be compatible with your approach.

Personal referrals have great value. Their drawback is that they limit you to what the members of your professional network know about evaluation researchers.

Contacting the state chapter of the American Evaluation Association

Most states have a chapter of the American Evaluation Association. Chapters are typically organized and managed by one or more evaluators who volunteer for this task. Chapters have lists of members, and most chapters will provide access to this list for people who want to hire an evaluation consultant.

Use of an American Evaluation Association chapter has the major advantage of linking you to a network of consultants wider than you probably could have identified on your own. However, as previously noted, membership in the American Evaluation Association does not indicate that a person has achieved any sort of certification. In addition, it does not imply any common set of standards or approaches to evaluation. The buyer must always beware!

Advertising through a request for proposals

Organizations seeking an evaluation consultant frequently issue requests for proposals (RFPs). They may send these to a few or a large number of consultants. Sometimes they obtain a mailing list from their state American Evaluation Association chapter for this purpose. Sometimes they solicit names and addresses by word of mouth. Occasionally, the use of an RFP is mandated by a funding body as a condition of receiving grant money for a program and an associated evaluation.

Developing and sending an RFP to prospective vendors of evaluation services has advantages for you and the consultant. For you, the process of developing the RFP and reviewing proposals you receive in response to it will help you clarify your expectations for the evaluation. You will receive information from interested consultants in a standard format that will facilitate apples-to-apples comparisons among different vendors. A good RFP enables consultants to know what you expect and approximately when you expect it. The RFP often gives them enough information to determine whether their interests and qualifications match the job. Thus, they can decide whether to consider the work without wasting your time and theirs trying to construct a general picture of what the project will entail.

Creating an RFP

The typical components of an RFP include:

- A description of your organization: name, location, size, mission.

- A description of the program to be evaluated: goals, major activities, number and types of persons who participate in it.

- A statement of the outcomes expected from the program, to the extent that you know them now. (You may develop or refine these with the consultant.)

- A summary description of the work you would like the evaluator to do. This part of the RFP provides the consultant with a general picture of your expectations, as you know them at the present time.

- Any practical considerations that will affect the consultant's decision whether to bid on the work and the consultant's decisions about the best approach to propose. These may include important deadlines, cost considerations, or special requirements your organization has for doing program evaluation research.

- Consultant qualifications, if you have any characteristics that you feel are essential.

- Submission requirements, including the person and address to which the proposal must be submitted, date by which the proposal must be submitted, maximum length (if any), and required format (if any).

Productive Use of Evaluation Consultants

Of course, the principles of good relationships that apply to your daily interaction also apply to relationships with evaluators. In addition, here is some specific advice, based on many years of observing good and bad dynamics between program managers and evaluation researchers.

- Have a program theory. You don't have to have a perfectly formed theory before you start working with an evaluator. In fact, you could build one as part of your work together. However, you should be committed to having such a theory, because it will instantly communicate much of what the evaluator needs to know about things that need to be measured. Also, it will enhance your thinking about your program and, consequently, your ability to communicate both with the evaluator and with others.

- Intend to *use* the results of the evaluation. Develop a conscious plan for this, if possible. You will greatly increase the productivity of the evaluation if you keep your eye on how you want to use the results. This will improve the quality of your input into the design.

- Make your expectations as clear as possible. Clarify what the project should accomplish. If you have unclear expectations, you will likely achieve only frustration.

- Develop a good advisory committee (if appropriate). Advisory committees can inject insight and energy into projects. By having representatives from groups expected to use the information, you ensure that the design addresses their needs.

- Consider every step to be a collaborative work in progress. The more you work together with the evaluator, the more likely that your needs will be met and the evaluation product will be useful.

- Focus on the information needs of the users of the project's results. Make sure that you have considered what all intended users want to get from the study.[20]

- Budget enough time (for the design and for the work itself). It is common, especially among people who have little experience with evaluation, to grossly underestimate the amount of time it will take to design and implement good evaluation research. Each of the steps listed in Chapter 3 requires time.

- Budget enough money (as discussed in the next section). As a general principle, it is important to provide adequate financial resources to fulfill the goals you have for the evaluation.

- Develop clear and reasonable standards for communication and progress reports. Specify how you would like to communicate with the evaluator, the content of the communication, and how often you would like updates on progress.

- Realize there will be some ambiguity. No matter what, some degree of imprecision will always exist in this work. Not everything can be neatly tied down, planned, and explained. Results will rarely, if ever, lead to absolutely clear-cut interpretations and recommendations.

---

[20] Michael Quinn Patton, one of the foremost authorities on evaluation, stresses in his writings and talks the importance of emphasizing "intended uses by intended users." See his *Utilization-Focused Evaluation* (Thousand Oaks, CA: Sage, 1997).

What Does Program Evaluation Cost?

Asking how much evaluation costs is a bit like asking, "How much does a house cost?" The answer, obviously, depends on exactly what you want, where you want it, and when you want it. So, this section offers some principles you can apply as you consider costs.

Evaluation research, as we have seen, can involve:

- Gathering a little bit of information (lower cost) or a lot of information (higher cost).
- Use of existing information (lower cost) or use of new information (higher cost).
- Use of methods capable of measuring only major results (lower cost) or use of detailed, sensitive methods capable of measuring small and unique results (higher cost).

Another consideration is the time period over which you want to amortize costs. For example, what is the cost of purchasing better insulation for your house? If you look only at the cost of the insulation during the year you install it, the expense might seem large. On the other hand, if you examine your heating costs over the next five years, you may find that you save more in heat bills than you paid for the insulation, so the "cost" is actually a "savings" — real money in your pocket, not a subtraction from your bank account. Ways that evaluation research can save you money or increase your revenues appeared in the discussion of the benefits of evaluation in Chapter 1. They include making programs more effective and efficient, improving your ability to obtain grants and contracts, and improving your image. Each of these benefits directly or indirectly improves your financial position.

The next few pages contain some observations that might be helpful as you consider the cost of evaluation.

An example, with costs

Let's take a hypothetical example, and then we can discuss what this example shows us. The example involves "PeopleServ, Inc.," a nonprofit organization that has decided to work with a nonprofit research organization.

PeopleServ, Inc., is a program that provides employment training and placement services to hard-to-employ individuals. PeopleServ serves about 1,200 people each year. It would like a one-time evaluation to understand the effectiveness of its program, and how its services can improve.

PeopleServ wants to answer the following questions:

- What percentage of clients complete the program?
- Do certain types of clients have a better record of completing the program than others do?
- How satisfied are clients with the services they receive?
- What proportion of clients obtain jobs?
- Are certain types of clients more likely than others to obtain jobs?
- What are the wages for the jobs obtained by clients? Are these wages enough to keep them above the poverty level?
- How many clients who get jobs stay in them for at least six months?

To answer these questions to its satisfaction, PeopleServ and its evaluation consultant, with input from an advisory committee, decide that the evaluation requires:

- Organization and tallying of enrollment and participation records
- Follow-up interviews with two hundred clients when they leave the program and six months after they leave
- Follow-up interviews with fifty program "dropouts"

Tables 1, 2, and 3 indicate some time and cost features of this project.

Table 1 describes how much time the evaluation consulting organization may require to complete the work within each of the four phases of the project. These figures are conservative, based on the experiences of many organizations in this situation—organizations that had not previously set up a system for evaluation.

Table 1. Time Required for Project

Phase of work	Some activities for the evaluator*	Time requirements (conservative estimate)
Design	• Three meetings with staff, including preparation and travel • One meeting with advisory committee, including preparation and travel • Selection of measurement instruments • Brief review of literature • Drafting and redrafting of design, with procedures	• Evaluation researcher: 40 hours • Evaluation assistant: 24 hours • Secretary: 10 hours
Data Collection	• Overseeing and implementing procedures • Tracking survey respondents, based on last available information • Conducting interviews • Editing and coding completed interviews • Storing data in database	• Interviewer supervisor: 32 hours • Evaluation assistant: 10 hours • Interviewers: 340 hours • Programmer: 8 hours
Analysis	• Statistical processing of information • Drafting of written report • Meeting with advisory committee	• Evaluation researcher: 32 hours • Evaluation assistant: 26 hours • Secretary: 10 hours
Reporting	• Issuing final report • Presentation to board of directors, including preparation of sophisticated graphics as requested by executive director • Extra presentation requested by funders	• Evaluation researcher: 16 hours • Evaluation assistant: 10 hours • Secretary: 8 hours

* For purposes of illustration, the table lists only some of the activities of the evaluator. There are more, as described in Chapter 3.

Table 2 lists probable staff costs for the work. Note that the table shows just wages, no other costs. Figures are based on salary surveys computing the average wage for people in the specified positions in a midwestern urban area. Wages will be higher in some parts of the country, and lower in others.

Table 2. Staff Costs

Staff	Hourly wage	Hours on project	Total wage cost
Evaluation researcher	$24.04	88	$2,115.38
Evaluation assistant	$15.87	70	$1,110.58
Secretary	$11.54	28	$323.08
Interviewers	$10.10	340	$3,432.69
Interviewer supervisor	$13.94	32	$446.15
Programmer	$23.08	8	$184.62
Total staff costs			**$7,612.50**

Table 3 adds staff costs to other costs, to calculate a total cost for the project. Note that these costs include the actual, direct costs that have to be paid to get the work done, plus overhead costs, such as supervision, training, vacation and sick time, and other items. Since this is a nonprofit organization, there is no cost included for profit.

Table 3. Total Costs

Item	Cost
Staff wages	$7,612
Benefits (15%)	$1,142
Printing	$500
Facilities and supplies (rent, phones, computer)	$1,665
Direct cost total	**$10,919**
Overhead (15%)	$1,638
Total costs	**$12,557**

This example can provide a reference point for you. You may envision an evaluation project for your organization that requires more hours or fewer hours. You may be located in a part of the world with higher or lower costs than those cited in the example. Because this organization had done no previous evaluation, design time was anticipated to be longer than for an organization with some experience. Nonetheless, the example provides excellent figures to help you think about potential costs in your own situation.

One more observation: not all costs depend equally on the size of the project. Some costs are relatively fixed. For example, it takes as much time to design a survey for fifty people as for five hundred people. It can take as much time to write a report based on a survey of five hundred people as for fifty people. Other costs vary with size; in the same example, follow-up phone calls to fifty people will be far less expensive than follow-up calls to five hundred.

Summary

This chapter has covered practical issues related to staffing and cost. No single answer exists for the question, Who should do the evaluation research? nor for the question, How much will the evaluation cost? Different options have different advantages and disadvantages. Different options have different costs. Different options suit different organizations, depending on their skills, resources, and preferences. Even within one organization, management might decide to take diverse approaches to the evaluation of various programs.

The final chapter of this book explores ways you can be sure the evaluation you conduct is believable and shows that the work you do makes a difference.

5

How Can We Show We Are Making a Difference?

One morning, a public radio station unashamedly announced the results of their "unscientific" poll: 58 percent of the people who telephoned that morning to voice their opinion about a particular policy agreed with that policy. Some listeners, I am certain, accepted this "unscientifically gathered" information as the truth as readily as if it had been "scientifically gathered." I was frustrated that a station I admire would "cheat," that is, that they would create the impression that they had a sampling of public opinion, when in fact they did not (but they could always defend themselves through their claim that they had labeled their findings "unscientific").

What exactly separates "scientific information" from other forms of information? What makes information credible and "valid"? What makes the interpretations and conclusions we draw from a study "correct"? Even in the natural sciences, these are perplexing questions.[21]

Many evaluation texts state that to show cause and effect you need to set up experimental designs, identify "control groups," and engage in other "scientific procedures." But strategic management judgments about programs and policies are a blend of scientific reasoning, politics, values, and common sense. Your job is not to find the "truth"; it is not to meet some abstract criteria of "science." Rather, your job is to make sure your evaluation study is *believable* to people to whom the study matters, and can withstand sincere,

---

[21] See, for example, A. F. Chalmers, *What Is This Thing Called Science?* (Buckingham, UK: Open University Press, 1999) for a discussion of what makes science science.

reasonable challenges. Your task is to make the results of your work *as credible as possible to the greatest number of relevant people.*

So, what exactly does that mean? If you want to show you make a difference, if you want to claim that your program or service produced an important positive change in the community, if you want to reassure yourself, your board, your funders, and your consumers that you are doing the right thing, how can you ensure that your evaluation work includes whatever features it requires to fulfill your needs?

Guidelines for making the results of your work as credible as possible to the greatest number of people appear in Figure 13. Remember, we are just trying to increase the probability that people will accept your findings and conclusions. In a realm that includes politics and values, no guarantees exist.

We have touched on most of the guidelines in Figure 13 already, in Chapter 2. One of them, having a "comparison," is a topic we have not discussed. We will spend some time on it here.

Figure 13. Guidelines for Credible Findings

Guideline	Reason why it is important
Show your work.	Many of us heard this frequently from our mathematics teachers. It pertains to evaluation research as well. If people can see the methods you used and can examine data on their own, they can assess what you did and feel confident about your conclusions. Many evaluation studies do not afford this opportunity to their readers, and the credibility of these studies suffers as a result.
Include the four essential types of evaluation information: client, service data, documentation of results, and perceptions (see Figure 3, p. 17).	If you have this information, you will be in a strong position to provide a portrait of what you are doing, and to respond to any requests about or challenges to your findings.

Figure 13. Guidelines for Credible Findings (continued)

Guideline	Reason why it is important
Match your method to your conclusions.	If you are at an early stage of exploring how your program is working, it's fine to talk to an easily assembled number of participants (a "convenience sample") to get some preliminary feedback. Or if you just want to obtain suggestions for improvements to the program, it's fine to schedule some focus groups for whoever can show up. The information can be meaningful, and it can lead to productive changes.
	On the other hand, if you want to confirm that you are effective and making a difference, you'll need to draw a more inclusive sample. You'll need to measure things in a way that both you and other readers of the evaluation findings can count numbers and see improvements. So, for example, if you and others are concerned about barriers that keep people from obtaining your service, it would be reasonable to remain skeptical of any findings that included only the opinions of people who come in your door. You need to talk with people who can't get there or people who might have dropped out.
Include some sort of program theory.	People accept cause-and-effect conclusions more readily if the conclusions fit within a reasonable framework that lets everyone know why things happen the way they do. The discussion of program theories (pages 21–32) showed that techniques such as logic models can provide coherence and context that strengthen the credibility of findings.
Include enough participants in your study.	A case study of one person who receives services from your program can be very enlightening and worthwhile. Unfortunately, it won't convince most reasonable people that your service is effective. It also does not allow you to identify any differences that might exist among different types of people who come into your program. Larger numbers are more acceptable to more people who want to use evaluation results to shape programs and policies and to make funding decisions. Conclusions from a study with 250 participants will, on average, be accepted by more people than conclusions from a study with 25 participants.
Have a comparison.	The strongest evidence of cause and effect, for reasonable people, is a good comparison.

Developing a credible comparison

Presumably, you expect that your program will produce some outcomes. Let's say that 80 percent of the participants in your program do, in fact, achieve those outcomes. Can you claim that four out of five people receiving your service benefit from it and achieve the desired outcomes? Most of you have the experience to know that you cannot make that claim. It's quite possible that 80 percent of the participants might have achieved those outcomes anyway, without any help from your program. Possession of information based solely on people who received your service does not provide you with the strongest possible evidence of program impacts.

Figure 14. Credible Comparisons for Program Evaluations

Comparison	Value
Comparing service recipients "to themselves" over time	This is the weakest form of comparison, but it's still better than nothing. It requires taking an initial measure to establish a baseline, and then taking one or more measurements later, either while they are receiving your service or immediately after their participation in the program. This procedure offers the opportunity to provide evidence that the people's situation improved, or that they had their needs met. This can support the supposition that such improvement might have occurred because of your program. Moreover, if you can't detect any improvement, you have obtained some important information.
Comparing service recipients to people waiting for service	Often, people apply to take part in a program and have essentially identical needs and characteristics to those who participate in the program, but space doesn't allow the program to fit them in. These people can be a handy source of comparative information. If you can gather this information over a long enough time period, they become a reasonable comparison group to provide some evidence of the effectiveness of your program.

For this reason, many evaluation practitioners would say that you need a *control group.* For our purposes, a control group is a group of people who qualify for your service, but when they apply are randomly assigned not to receive the service, so you can observe how they differ over time from those who do receive the service. Control groups are valuable for some studies. For most evaluation research, however, control groups are not practical and, in fact, not necessary.

Remember, your task is to make the results of your work *as credible as possible to the greatest number of relevant people.* You need to identify some form of comparison that will supply sufficiently compelling evidence to the

Figure 14. Credible Comparisons (continued)

Comparison	Value
Comparing service recipients to similar individuals in the general population	Your community may have many people who could benefit from your service but do not receive it. If you can contact them to obtain information, and if they don't differ from service recipients in any way that would call your analysis into question, then they may serve as a good comparison group.
Comparing service recipients to a group of people eligible for service who are randomly assigned not to receive it	This is the traditional control group in an experimental design. In the language of experimentalists, if you make this comparison, any differences you identify between service recipients and non-recipients have resulted only from (a) your impact and (b) chance fluctuations. If you feel confident that chance fluctuations are minimal, then you have produced strong evidence of the difference you have made.
Comparing service recipients in your program to service recipients in other programs	This technique can be fruitful, and it requires little extra effort on your part. If information exists about program completion rates, success rates (short-term or long-term), or any other characteristics of people who have participated in similar programs, then you have reference points against which to make some useful comparisons. Often, information from a variety of programs has been compiled and summarized and is available in books or journals. The major downside is that the information you need for a good comparison is frequently not available.

people who are the primary stakeholders or users of your study. In most cases, this will not require the inclusion of a control group in your evaluation research.

What sort of comparisons will strengthen your study and make it as credible as possible to the greatest number of people? In studies of programs that attempt to achieve outcomes with individuals or families, five types of comparison are credible. These are comparing service recipients to themselves over time, comparing them to people waiting for service, comparing them to similar people in the general population, comparing them to a control group, as described above, and comparing them to people in similar programs. These comparisons are described in Figure 14.

Summary

In a nutshell, if you want to claim credit for producing an outcome, you have to show that something changed and that it probably changed because of what you did. The best way to accomplish this is to have a strong, credible comparison. In this chapter, we have seen why this is important and have reviewed some ways to gather comparative data.

Conclusion:
Good Luck on the Evaluation Highway!

"I do now remember a saying: 'The fool doth think he is wise, but the wise man knows himself to be a fool.'"

> —Touchstone, the clown in Shakespeare's
> *As You Like It*. Act 5 Sc. 1.

You have reached the conclusion of this journey, but only the beginning of your further journeys related to evaluation and the improvement of the work that you and your organization carry out. Shakespeare said it well—that every door is an exit and also an entrance.[22] The final pages of this book are such a portal, sending you on your way to do and use program evaluation.

The word for the wise person, at this point, is *search*. The development of programs and policies that benefit people involves a constant search. We seriously err if we think we know it all, or if we remain rigid in our thinking and our approaches to addressing issues. We must strive for enough wisdom to "know ourselves to be fools." We must adopt the mentality of searching—always searching.

Program evaluation helps us to search effectively. Early in this book, we used "finding the best route to work" as an example of common sense, an

---

[22] Of course, as Brendan Behan pointed out, "Shakespeare said pretty well everything, and what he left out, James Joyce put in." Brendan Behan, *Brendan Behan's New York* (Boston: Little, Brown and Co., 1964), 123.

example of everyday thinking that illustrates the basic features of evaluation. In searching for the best route—indeed, in searching for anything in life—our instincts tell us to test, explore, look for better options. Evaluation helps us to do that, within the realm of programs and policies intended to better the lives of individuals, groups, and communities of any size.

The difference between program evaluation and common sense is that evaluation offers a systematic approach, including methods that have been refined over the years, to understanding and improving work. Evaluation, of course, is a process. It comprises part of a search, a search for better ways to do what we want to do.

Program evaluation enables us to represent our efforts and accomplishments to others. While we can't ever develop the capacity to convince all of the people all of the time, the principles in this book can be used to produce practical and credible information that you and others can use to improve programs and influence policies.

Program evaluation should not be treated as a win/lose activity. It does not authenticate a score and identify a winner, like the referee at the conclusion of a sporting event. Rather, it is part of an ongoing process of serving others, while searching for better ways to improve that service.

This book is one of many maps you will use in your search. It has provided a basic overview of evaluation, it has described how you can work with an evaluation professional, and it has offered advice on the recruitment and hiring of someone to do program evaluation work for you.

As you proceed with your journey, best of luck!

References

Altschuld, James W.
    1999   "The Certification of Evaluators: Highlights from a Report Submitted to the Board of Directors of the American Evaluation Association." *American Journal of Evaluation* 20: 481–93.

Behan, Brendan
    1964   *Brendan Behan's New York.* Boston: Little, Brown and Co.

Bickman, Leonard, and Debra J. Rog, eds.
    1998   *Handbook of Applied Social Research Methods.* Thousand Oaks, CA: Sage.

Caracelli, Valerie J., and Hallie Preskill
    2000   *The Expanding Scope of Evaluation Use.* San Francisco: Jossey-Bass.

Chalmers, A. F.
    1999   *What Is This Thing Called Science?* Buckingham, UK: Open University Press.

Hosley, Cheryl
    2000   *Strategies for Measuring Accessibility of Mental Health Programs.* Saint Paul, MN: Amherst H. Wilder Foundation.

Iwaniec, Dorothy, and John Pinkerton, eds.
1998   *Making Research Work.* Chichester, England: John Wiley & Sons.

Jones, Steven C., and Blaine R. Worthen
1999   "AEA Members' Opinions Concerning Evaluator Certification." *American Journal of Evaluation* 20: 495–506.

Lévi-Strauss, Claude
1966   *The Savage Mind.* Chicago: University of Chicago Press.

Mattessich, Paul W.
2001   "Lessons Learned: What These Seven Studies Teach Us." *Cancer Practice* 9: 78–84.

Mattessich, Paul W., Donald W. Compton, and Michael Baizerman
2001   "Evaluation Use and the Collaborative Evaluation Fellows Project." *Cancer Practice* 9: 85–91.

Mattessich, Paul W., and Barbara R. Monsey
1998   *Stating Outcomes for American Cancer Society Programs.* Atlanta, GA: American Cancer Society.

Mattessich, Paul W., Marta Murray-Close, and Barbara R. Monsey
2001   *Collaboration: What Makes It Work.* 2d ed. Saint Paul, MN: Fieldstone Alliance.

Mida, Kristine L.
1996   *Program Outcome Evaluation.* Milwaukee, WI: Families International.

Patton, Michael Quinn
1997   *Utilization-Focused Evaluation.* Thousand Oaks, CA: Sage.

Pecora, Peter J., Mark W. Fraser, Kristine E. Nelson, Jacquelyn McCroskey, and William Meezan
1995   *Evaluating Family-Based Services.* New York: Aldine De Gruyter.

Rogers, Patricia J., Anthony Petrosino, Tracy A. Huebner, and Timothy A. Hacsi
    2000   "Program Theory Evaluation: Practice, Promise, and Problems."
           In *Program Theory in Evaluation: Challenges and Opportunities,* Patricia J. Rogers, Timothy A. Hacsi, Anthony Petrosino, and Tracy A. Huebner, eds., 5–13. San Francisco: Jossey-Bass.

Smith, Michael J.
    1990   *Program Evaluation in the Human Services.* New York: Springer.

United Way of America
    1996   *Measuring Program Outcomes: A Practical Approach.* Alexandria, VA: United Way of America.

Index

More results-oriented books from Fieldstone Alliance

Boards

The Best of the Board Café
Hands-on Solutions for Nonprofit Boards

by Jan Masaoka, CompassPoint Nonprofit Services

Gathers the most requested articles from the e-newsletter, *Board Café*. You'll find a lively menu of ideas, information, opinions, news, and resources to help board members give and get the most out of their board service.

232 pp • Item 069407 • ISBN 978-0-940069-40-4

The Nonprofit Board Member's Guide to Lobbying and Advocacy

by Marcia Avner

Board members are uniquely positioned to be effective and influential lobbyists. This guide spells out how your board can use their power and privilege to move your nonprofit's work forward.

128 pp • Item 069393 • ISBN 978-0-940069-39-8

Collaboration

Collaboration Handbook
Creating, Sustaining, and Enjoying the Journey

by Michael Winer and Karen Ray

Shows you how to get a collaboration going, set goals, determine everyone's roles, create an action plan, and evaluate the results. Includes a case study of one collaboration from start to finish, helpful tips on how to avoid pitfalls, and worksheets to keep everyone on track.

192 pp • Item 069032 • ISBN 978-0-940069-03-9

Collaboration: What Makes It Work, 2nd Ed.

by Paul Mattessich, PhD, Marta Murray-Close, BA, and Barbara Monsey, MPH

An in-depth review of current collaboration research. Major findings are summarized, critical conclusions are drawn, and twenty key factors influencing successful collaborations are identified. Includes *The Wilder Collaboration Factors Inventory,* which groups can use to assess their collaboration.

104 pp • Item 069326 • ISBN 978-0-940069-32-9

The Nimble Collaboration
Fine-Tuning Your Collaboration for Lasting Success

by Karen Ray

Shows you ways to make your existing collaboration more responsive, flexible, and productive. Provides three key strategies to help your collaboration respond quickly to changing environments and participants.

136 pp • Item 069288 • ISBN 978-0-940069-28-2

Community Building

Community Building: What Makes It Work

by Wilder Research

Reveals twenty-eight keys to help you build community more effectively. Includes detailed descriptions of each factor, case examples of how they play out, and practical questions to assess your work.

112 pp • Item 069121 • ISBN 978-0-940069-12-1

The Community Economic Development Handbook
Strategies and Tools to Revitalize Your Neighborhood

by Mihailo Temali

A concrete, practical handbook to turning any neighborhood around. It explains how to start a community economic development organization, and then lays out the steps of four proven and powerful strategies for revitalizing inner-city neighborhoods.

288 pp • Item 069369 • ISBN 978-0-940069-36-7

Community Leadership Handbook
Framing Ideas, Building Relationships, and Mobilizing Resources

by James F. Krile with Gordon Curphy and Duane R. Lund

Leadership is a choice, not a position. You can improve your community, and this hands-on guide shows you how. Based on the best of Blandin Foundation's 20-year experience in developing community leaders, it gives community members—like yourself—the tools to bring people together to make changes.

216 pp • Item 069547 • ISBN 978-0-940069-54-1

Visit **www.FieldstoneAlliance.org** to learn more about these and many other books on community building, nonprofit management, and funder capacity. You can also sign up to receive our free "Tools You Can Use" e-newsletter and find out about our consulting services. Call 1-800-274-6024 for a current catalog.

The Fieldstone Alliance Nonprofit Field Guide to
Conducting Community Forums

by Carol Lukas and Linda Hoskins

Provides step-by-step instruction to plan and carry out exciting, successful community forums that will educate the public, build consensus, focus action, or influence policy.

128 pp • Item 069318 • ISBN 978-0-940069-31-2

The Creative Community Builder's Handbook
How to Transform Communities Using Local Assets, Arts, and Culture

by Tom Borrup

Art and culture can be a powerful catalyst for revitalizing the economic, social, and physical conditions in communities. This handbook gives you successful strategies, best practices, and "how-to" guidance to turn cultural gems into effective community change.

280 pp • Item 069474 • ISBN 978-0-940069-47-3

Crossing Borders, Sharing Journeys
Effective Capacity Building with Immigrant and Refugee Groups

by Sarah Gleason

This report outlines seven broad factors found to contribute to effective capacity building with immigrant and refugee lead organizations (IRLOs). Case studies illustrate practices used when working with IRLOs and highlights principles that other capacity builders can apply when working with similar groups. You can also download a free copy of this report at www.Fieldstone-Alliance.org.

88 pp • Item 069628 • ISBN 978-0-940069-62-6

New Americans, New Promise
A Guide to the Refugee Journey in America

by Yorn Yan

Gain a better understanding of the refugee experience in the U.S. Refugee-serving organizations will find solid, practical advice for how to best help refugees through the acculturation and transition process of becoming a New American. Refugees will discover what to expect during five stages of development that they typically progress through as they adapt to their new home.

200 pp • Item 069504 • ISBN 978-0-940069-50-3

Finance

Bookkeeping Basics
What Every Nonprofit Bookkeeper Needs to Know

by Debra L. Ruegg and Lisa M. Venkatrathnam

Complete with step-by-step instructions, a glossary of accounting terms, detailed examples, and handy reproducible forms, this book will enable you to successfully meet the basic bookkeeping requirements of your nonprofit organization—even if you have little or no formal accounting training.

128 pp • Item 069296 • ISBN 978-0-940069-29-9

Coping with Cutbacks
The Nonprofit Guide to Success When Times Are Tight

by Emil Angelica and Vincent Hyman

Shows you practical ways to involve business, government, and other nonprofits to solve problems together. Also includes 185 cutback strategies you can put to use right away.

128 pp • Item 069091 • ISBN 978-0-940069-09-1

Financial Leadership for Nonprofit Executives
Guiding Your Organization to Long-term Success

by Jeanne Bell and Elizabeth Schaffer

Gives the Executive Director the framework, specific language, and processes needed to lead with confidence and create an effective nonprofit business that strikes the balance between mission and money.

152 pp • Item 06944X • ISBN 978-0-940069-44-2

Venture Forth!
The Essential Guide to Starting a Moneymaking Business in Your Nonprofit Organization

by Rolfe Larson

The most complete guide on nonprofit business development. Building on the experience of dozens of organizations, this handbook gives you a time-tested approach for finding, testing, and launching a successful nonprofit business venture.

272 pp • Item 069245 • ISBN 978-0-940069-24-4

Funder's Guides

Community Visions, Community Solutions
Grantmaking for Comprehensive Impact

by Joseph A. Connor and Stephanie Kadel-Taras

Helps foundations, community funds, government agencies, and other grantmakers uncover a community's highest aspiration for itself, and support and sustain strategic efforts to get to workable solutions.

128 pp • Item 06930X • ISBN 978-0-940069-30-5

A Funder's Guide to Evaluation
Leveraging Evaluation to Improve Nonprofit Effectiveness

by Peter York

Shifts away from using evaluation to prove something to someone else, and toward improving what nonprofits do so they can achieve their mission and share how they succeeded with others.

160 pp • Item 069482 • ISBN 978-0-940069-48-0

A Funder's Guide to Organizational Assessment
Tools, Processes, and Their Use in Building Capacity

Editor: Lori Bartczak

Funders, grantees, and consultants will understand how organizational assessment can be used to 1) Build the capacity of nonprofits, 2) Enhance grantmaking, 3) Impact organizational systems, 4) Strengthen the non-profit sector, and 5) Measure foundation effectiveness. The guide presents four grantee assessment tools and two tools for assessing foundation performance.

216 pp • Item 069539 • ISBN 978-0-940069-53-4
Includes CD-ROM with examples and adaptations of tools

Power in Policy
A Funder's Guide to Advocacy and Civic Participation

Editor: David F. Arons

Increasingly, foundations are finding that participation in public decision making is often a critical component in reaching the impact demanded by mission-related goals. For those weighing precisely what role foundations should play, the mix of real-life examples, practical advice, and inspiration in this book are invaluable.

320 pp • Item 069458 • ISBN 978-0-940069-45-9

Strengthening Nonprofit Performance
A Funder's Guide to Capacity Building

by Paul Connolly and Carol Lukas

This practical guide synthesizes the most recent capacity building practice and research into a collection of strategies, steps, and examples that you can use to get started on or improve funding to strengthen nonprofit organizations.

176 pp • Item 069377 • ISBN 978-0-940069-37-4

Lobbing, Advocacy, and Organizing

The Lobbying and Advocacy Handbook for Nonprofit Organizations
Shaping Public Policy at the State and Local Level

by Marcia Avner

The Lobbying and Advocacy Handbook is a planning guide and resource for nonprofit organizations that want to influence issues that matter to them. This book will help you decide whether to lobby and then put plans in place to make it work.

240 pp • Item 069261 • ISBN 978-0-940069-26-8

The Nonprofit Board Member's Guide to Lobbying and Advocacy

by Marcia Avner

Written specifically for board members, this guide helps organizations increase their impact on policy decisions. It reveals how board members can be involved in planning for and implementing successful lobbying efforts.

96 pp • Item 069393 • ISBN 978-0-940069-39-8

Management & Planning

The Accidental Techie
Supporting, Managing, and Maximizing Your Nonprofit's Technology

by Sue Bennett

How to support and manage technology on a day-to-day basis including: setting up a help desk, developing an effective technology budget and implementation plan, working with consultants and management, handling viruses, creating a backup system and schedule, purchasing hardware and software, and more.

176 pp • Item 069490 • ISBN 978-0-940069-49-7

Benchmarking for Nonprofits
How to Measure, Manage, and Improve Performance

by Jason Saul

Benchmarking is the continuous process of measuring your organization against leaders to gain knowledge and insights that will help you improve. This book defines a formal, systematic, and reliable way to benchmark—from preparing your organization to measuring performance and implementing best practices.

144 pp • Item 069431 • ISBN 978-0-940069-43-5

Consulting with Nonprofits
A Practitioner's Guide

by Carol A. Lukas

A step-by-step, comprehensive guide for consultants. Addresses the art of consulting, how to run your business, and much more. Also includes tips and anecdotes from thirty skilled consultants.

240 pp • Item 069172 • ISBN 978-0-940069-17-6

The Fieldstone Alliance Nonprofit Field Guide to
Developing Effective Teams

by Beth Gilbertsen and Vijit Ramchandani

Helps you understand, start, and maintain a team. Provides tools and techniques for writing a mission statement, setting goals, conducting effective meetings, creating ground rules to manage team dynamics, making decisions in teams, creating project plans, and developing team spirit.

80 pp • Item 069202 • ISBN 978-0-940069-20-6

The Five Life Stages of Nonprofit Organizations
Where You Are, Where You're Going, and What to Expect When You Get There

by Judith Sharken Simon with J. Terence Donovan

Shows you what's "normal" for each development stage which helps you plan for transitions, stay on track, and avoid unnecessary struggles. Includes *The Nonprofit Life Stage Assessment* to plot your organization's progress in seven arenas of organization development.

128 pp • Item 069229 • ISBN 978-0-940069-22-0

Generations
The Challenge of a Lifetime for Your Nonprofit

by Peter Brinckerhoff

What happens when a management team of all Baby Boomers leaves within a five-year stretch? The clock is ticking . . . . is your nonprofit ready? In this book, nonprofit mission expert Peter Brinckerhoff tells you what generational changes to expect and how to plan for them. You'll find in-depth information for each area of your organization—staff, board, volunteers, clients, marketing, technology, and finances.

232 pp • Item 069555 • ISBN 978-0-940069-55-8

Information Gold Mine
Innovative Uses of Evaluation

by Paul W. Mattessich, Shelly Hendricks, Ross VeLure Roholt

Don't underestimate the power of your evaluation findings. The real-life stories in this book clearly show the power of using evaluation data to produce good things for your nonprofit.

128 pp • Item 069512 • ISBN 978-0-940069-51-0

The Manager's Guide to Program Evaluation:
Planning, Contracting, and Managing for Useful Results

by Paul W. Mattessich, Ph.D.

Explains how to plan and manage an evaluation that will help identify your organization's successes, share information with key audiences, and improve services.

96 pp • Item 069385 • ISBN 978-0-940069-38-1

The Nonprofit Mergers Workbook Part I
The Leader's Guide to Considering, Negotiating, and Executing a Merger

by David La Piana

Save time, money, and untold frustration with this highly practical guide that makes the merger process manageable and controllable. Includes case studies, decision trees, twenty-two worksheets, checklists, tips, and complete step-by-step guidance.

240 pp • Item 069210 • ISBN 978-0-940069-21-3

The Nonprofit Mergers Workbook Part II
Unifying the Organization after a Merger

by La Piana Associates

Once the merger agreement is signed, the question becomes: How do we make this merger work? *Part II* helps you create a comprehensive plan to achieve *integration*—bringing together people, programs, processes, and systems from two (or more) organizations into a single, unified whole.

248 pp • Item 069415 • ISBN 978-0-940069-41-1
Includes CD-ROM with integration plan template

Nonprofit Stewardship
A Better Way to Lead Your Mission-Based Organization

by Peter Brinckerhoff

This guide outlines eight characteristics of a mission-based steward and gives you specific applications of stewardship—in planning and finance, risk-taking, and crisis management.

272 pp • Item 069423 • ISBN 978-0-940069-42-8

Resolving Conflict in Nonprofit Organizations
The Leader's Guide to Finding Constructive Solutions

by Marion Peters Angelica

Learn and practice conflict resolution skills, uncover and deal with the true issues, and design and conduct a conflict resolution process.

192 pp • Item 069164 • ISBN 978-0-940069-16-9

Strategic Planning Workbook for Nonprofit Organizations, Revised and Updated

by Bryan Barry

Chart a wise course for your nonprofit's future. This time-tested workbook gives you practical step-by-step guidance, real-life examples, and easy-to-use worksheets.

120 pp • Item 069075 • ISBN 978-0-940069-07-7
Includes CD-ROM with worksheets and templates

Marketing & Fundraising

The Fieldstone Alliance Nonprofit Field Guide to
Conducting Successful Focus Groups

by Judith Sharken Simon

Shows how to collect valuable information without a lot of money or special expertise. Using this proven technique, you'll get essential opinions and feedback to help you check out your assumptions, do better strategic planning, improve services or products, and more.

80 pp • Item 069199 • ISBN 978-0-940069-19-0

Marketing Workbook for Nonprofit Organizations Volume I: Develop the Plan

by Gary J. Stern

Don't just wish for results—get them! Here's how to create a straightforward, usable marketing plan. Includes the six Ps of Marketing, how to use them effectively, a sample marketing plan, tips on using the Internet, and worksheets.

208 pp • Item 069253 • ISBN 978-0-940069-25-1

Marketing Workbook for Nonprofit Organizations Volume II: Mobilize People for Marketing Success

by Gary J. Stern

Put together a successful promotional campaign based on the most persuasive tool of all: personal contact. Learn how to mobilize your entire organization, its staff, volunteers, and supporters in a focused, one-to-one marketing campaign.

192 pp • Item 069105 • ISBN 978-0-940069-10-7

Message Matters
Succeeding at the Crossroads of Mission and Market

by Rebecca Leet

Today, being heard demands delivering information that resonates with your audience's desires quickly, clearly, and continually. Message Matters gives you a simple framework for developing and using strategic messages so you can connect more successfully with your target audiences and compel them to action.

160 pp • Item 069636 • ISBN 978-0-940069-63-3

ORDERING INFORMATION

Order by phone, fax or online

Call toll-free: 800-274-6024
Internationally: 651-556-4509

Fax: 651-556-4517

E-mail: books@fieldstonealliance.org
Online: www.FieldstoneAlliance.org

Pricing and discounts

For current prices and discounts, please visit our web site at www.FieldstoneAlliance.org or call toll free at 800-274-6024.

Our NO-RISK guarantee

If you aren't completely satisfied with any book for any reason, simply send it back within 30 days for a full refund.

Quality assurance

We strive to make sure that all the books we publish are helpful and easy to use. Our major workbooks are tested and critiqued by experts before being published. Their comments help shape the final book and—we trust—make it more useful to you.

Do you have a book idea?

Fieldstone Alliance seeks manuscripts and proposals for books in the fields of nonprofit management and community development. To get a copy of our author guidelines, please call us at 800-274-6024. You can also download them from our web site at www.FieldstoneAlliance.org

Visit us online

You'll find information about Fieldstone Alliance and more details on our books, such as table of contents, pricing, discounts, endorsements, and more, at www.FieldstoneAlliance.org